Culture Matters

'Every single day brings new challenges for the world of retail. As an industry, we are at the forefront of changes in customer behaviours. We have seen probably more disruption than most other sectors. A carefully defined culture is the constant that enables organisations to get ahead of change, even in a crisis.'

Paul Kelly, Lifelong retailer

'Having made a number of acquisitions in recent years, we prioritised culture as the golden thread to bring all businesses together. Alan O'Neill navigated us in embracing and tailoring the guiding principles outlined in this book. They have made a big impact on our customers and our own teams.'

Jan Patrick Schulz, CEO Landbell Group

'As the internal lead for a culture refresh programme in our multi-national group, we engaged Alan O'Neill for external support. His empathy for the business and our people was refreshing. His clarity of thought and practical approach made the journey a lot easier. What I particularly like about Alan's approach is how he links culture to real commercial results. I can relate to so many of the anecdotes outlined in this book.'

Martin Tobin, CEO European Recycling Platform, Ireland

'In the twenty-first century, culture has changed its spelling. Kulcha is the escape from culture. It's local. It's informal. It's grassroots digital. And it's genderless. I have known Alan for 20 years and worked side by side with him on a number of projects. His passion for people and culture flows through these pages. I have seen first-hand how he influences the leaders of iconic brands to put customer and people first. He gets it!'

Paco Underhill, author, speaker, observer, traveller

'Competing businesses often have the same levers available to attract customers and unlock growth. But time and again, it's the company that truly harnesses the power of its people to create empowered, motivated and purposeful teams that win out. Their superglue is an authentic culture. This parable of modern business culture unfolds on a cruise on the ancient River Shannon in Ireland. Just as folklore and heritage informs a nation's culture, this book illustrates through great storytelling how an organisation's culture will shape its business for years to come. We know we cannot change the past. But we can certainly influence our future, and this book shows us how.'

Paul Keeley, Director Regional Development at Fáilte Ireland

'As one of the oldest companies in Dubai, heritage and culture are very important to us. The four values outlined by Alan in this book resonate with us too. We put customers at the heart of all we do and we pride ourselves on our great people. As a leader in a fast-moving industry, we must continue to be agile in order to sustain our success.'

Tarek El Sakka, CEO Dubai Refreshments

'As a large public sector organisation, we pride ourselves in placing the customer at the heart of everything we do. Creating the right working environment is important to us and we were delighted to have had Alan O'Neill support and challenge us in our journey. The definition I particularly like is "culture is what happens when leaders are not around." At DVLA we place great importance in our leaders recognising, involving, developing and supporting their teams. We feel that these four ingredients are vital in creating a trusting environment where our people feel valued.'

Jonathan Matthews, Head of OCSD Central Support, DVLA

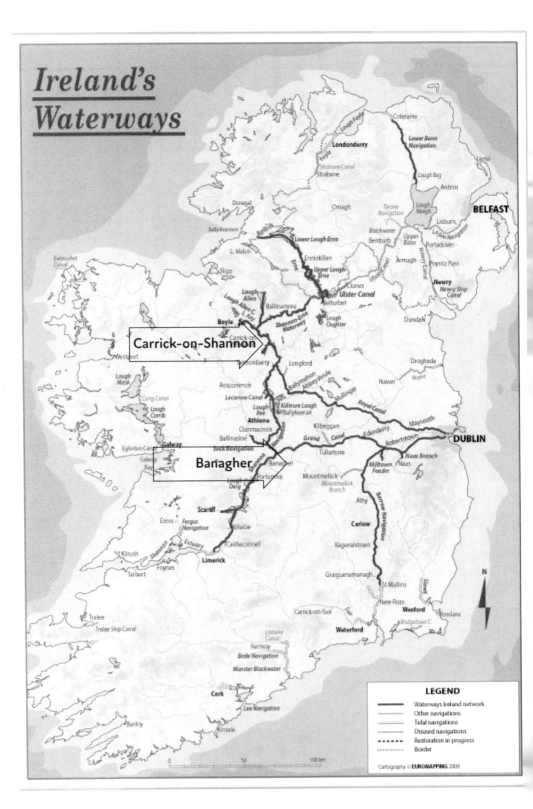

© Waterways Ireland

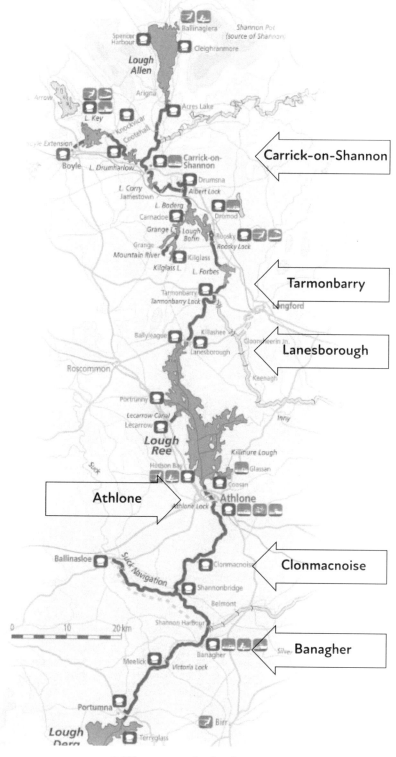

© Waterways Ireland

Culture Matters

The Four "Must-Have" Values to
Supercharge Your Business

ALAN O'NEILL

ORPEN PRESS

Published by
Orpen Press
Upper Floor, Unit B3
Hume Centre
Hume Avenue
Park West Industrial Estate
Dublin 12

email: info@orpenpress.com
www.orpenpress.com

© Alan O'Neill, 2021

Paperback ISBN 978-1-78605-135-6
ePub ISBN 978-1-78605-136-3

Printed in Dublin by SPRINTprint Ltd

'To make change stick – create a new culture.'

John P. Kotter

ABOUT THE AUTHOR

Alan O'Neill is a consultant, author and keynote speaker specialising in change management, organisational culture and customer experience. For over 30 years, he has worked with some of the top companies around the world. He has supported iconic brands like Toyota, Getty Images, Harrods of London, the United Nations, Dubai Duty Free, Primark, Intel, Moët Chandon and others with his '7 Steps to Profit'.

Alan has lots of no-nonsense expertise with plenty to say. With tailored keynotes on the 7 Steps to Profit, change management, culture or customer experience, Alan has a reputation for making the complex simple ... being down-to-earth and practical ... with a commercial focus that brings everything back to the customer.

A visiting professor with ESA Business School Beirut, Alan also writes for several publications, including a weekly business advice column for the *Sunday Independent Business* – Ireland's leading business newspaper. He is the author of *Premium Is the New Black: In a world of dynamic change put customer experience at the heart of your decision-making* (Orpen Press, 2018).

With his tried and trusted 7 Steps to Profit, Alan's mission is to inspire others to maximise their potential, with commercial growth strategies that are practical and relevant.

alanoneill.biz

ALAN'S 7 STEPS TO PROFIT

What is it that has made famous global organisations so powerful and successful in their respective fields? What are their secrets to success?

They all have one thing in common and it's not that difficult! They all...

1. Follow a very structured path to excellence that Alan describes as the *7 Steps to Profit*
2. Manage *change* effectively with a highly structured framework
3. Have a strong and engaging organisational *culture*
4. Put *customer-experience* at the heart of all decision-making

For example, voted the best department store in the world and founded by American, Gordon Selfridge, Alan's *7 Steps to Profit* supported Selfridges in growing profit from £45m to £200m in a short number of years and to win multiple '*best department store in the world*' awards.

But it's not just about retail, whether its Financial Services, FMCG, Hospitality, Industrial, IT, Manufacturing, Motor, Retail, Telcos, Tourism to Travel, B2B–B2C, Alan's *7 Steps* will work for any organisation with an ambition to be the best in their field.

Alan is a proud Irishman, living in Dublin, and working all over the world.

Contact Alan at alanoneill.biz

* To engage Alan to speak at your event
* To access a suite of online programmes in Kara Academy
* To access the free *Culture Matters* online programme, go to https://courses.kara.ie/

For KARA, btts

ACKNOWLEDGEMENTS

I couldn't have written this book without the experiences I have had working with so many amazing organisations around the world. While I had the enormous privilege of supporting your businesses, I also learned a great deal from each of you. There is no perfect formula for success for any business, regardless of the industry it is in. Consultants like me can advise with all sorts of business models, best practices and ingredients for success. But they all have to be interpreted and adapted and then applied by you. Each of you has your own unique heritage, people, culture, opportunities and challenges. So it's through a meeting of our collective minds that we can ensure the best route for you to follow.

I didn't go to the top of a mountain and come down with these four "must-have" values, having created them from my research or from figments of my imagination. They came from you. So, thank you.

I want to acknowledge what I learned from the four characters that inspired the name *Strudwick*. The 'S' comes from Tom Smith, my first boss, who taught me about buying for a pound and selling for two. He also taught this seventeen year-old how to respect others. Our friendship lasted for 36 years. And I still miss him.

Gerry Dalton gave me the 'D'. He taught me about systems, commitment and long hours. I also bought my first business from Gerry having learned from him how to be a professional manager.

The 'W' is a nod to Pearse Walsh, who welcomed me into a world that I didn't even know existed. The world of *training* was as alien to me as the world of writing proposals, charging for my time and intellectual property. I learned from his relaxed style how to facilitate workshops with people of all types. And I've never looked back since. He and I supported each other

Acknowledgements

as we both studied for our MBAs. We also owned a great business together called Harvest Resources, which has since gone from strength to strength with different owners.

The 'K' in Strudwick refers to Paul Kelly. I have known Paul for 30 years and have supported him as a consultant with various projects in that time. That started initially when he led A|Wear and Brown Thomas in Ireland. Later when he was appointed Managing Director of the iconic Selfridges in the UK, he invited me to support him with a significant change programme there that stretched across eight years. That was a resounding success as the Weston Family-owned business grew massively under his stewardship, winning multiple awards and smashing financial targets. A brilliant retailer with his finger permanently on the pulse of the wider market and his own business, he inspired great followership with his no-nonsense leadership style. And that included me too.

I also want to thank several people with the surname O'Neill. They include Anita, Anne, Finola, Kerrie and Ross. Your forensic edits and suggestions were challenging but appropriate. And I'll extend that to also include Paula Walsh, Marie Hennessy, Dara Breaden and the great team at Orpen Press.

Finally, I want to thank two mentors who now support and challenge their father every day. That's Kerrie and Ross. And I thought it was meant to be the other way around. How did that happen?

Alan O'Neill
Alanoneill.biz

CONTENTS

Contents

PREFACE

This book highlights the importance of culture and the need to proactively define your own unique culture. The thing is, you have a culture already. That culture is the beating heart of your business. It's a combination of attitudes, behaviours and processes. It's often described as 'the way we do things around here'. But is yours the right culture to deliver on your ambition? Is it fit for purpose in a dramatic and ever-changing world?

Covid-19 has turned our world upside down. What started off as a health crisis morphed into an economic crisis also. Global lockdowns, phased re-openings, social distancing, home-working and the digital explosion to online commerce became the norm for everyone. Adapting to dramatic change due to the ongoing threat of further lockdowns changed the dynamic as we knew it. All of that came on the back of the global financial crisis only a few years previously and the more recent geo-political unrest – examples include the Brexit vote and trade tariff wars between the US and China.

Businesses have to move fast to cope in these changing times. The military slogan, 'improvise, adapt and overcome' is a good mantra for our new world. There is no reference book to lean on, no precedent for managing in a pandemic. For individuals, handling uncertainty is described as having mental toughness. For a business however, I believe it's culture. That, in my view, is why your culture is so critical and it's your culture—more than anything else —that is tested in tough times.

Culture is Step 2 in my *7 Steps to Sustainable Profit*. When you have a clearly defined culture that is embedded in your way of doing things, it brings consistency, clarity and it enables the effective execution of your strategy. Here are my *7 Steps to Sustainable Profit*.

7 Steps to Profit

Sustainable Profit

7. **Execution** *Do and Review*

6. **Proposition** *Build your 3-legged Stool*

5. **Customer** *Connect to your Customer*

4. **People** *Develop your Team*

3. **Strategy** *Plot your Strategy*

2. **Culture** *Refresh your Culture*

1. **Brand DNA** *Find your North Star*

There is an abundance of research on the topic of culture. I'm particularly impressed by the work of Robert E. Quinn and Kim S. Cameron from the University of Michigan. Their intellectual approach describes four culture types driven by two dimensions. One dimension is the extent of your organisation's focus on the external environment versus an internal one. And the other dimension refers to how flexible or rigid your business model and practices are. As you can imagine, this can be plotted on a 2 x 2 matrix diagram that calls out four culture types. And it's a helpful way of showing culture in the big picture.

For me as a practicing change management consultant however, I like to focus on practical tools, while still keeping an eye on the big picture. In saying that, I'm a strong advocate of using values or guiding principles to drive the required behaviours, decisions and processes. And that's the focus of this book. I draw this reasoning from the countless culture refresh programmes that I have supported in a 30-year career as a change management consultant and keynote speaker. I also write regularly on the topic in my weekly column in Ireland's leading newspaper, the *Sunday Independent*, *Gulf Business* and various other publications.

My approach to the topic of culture outlines the four 'must-have' values in a business' culture. I base my ideas on the realities of our modern world, where *change* is the only constant. This is not just because of the Covid-19 pandemic. The world was already experiencing exponential disruptive growth in terms of the speed, volume and complexity of change. Covid-19 just accelerated those trajectories.

Take e-commerce for example. During the global lockdown, the online element of retail sales increased to approximately 33 percent of overall retail sales. It did fall back after the spike, as bricks and mortar stores re-opened. However a team in McKinsey (mckinsey.com/featured-insights) predict it will fall back to a new level that is higher than before the lockdown. They speculate that in the new world post-Covid, online will have accelerated by three to five years to the level previously forecasted for 2025. Not only does that require different business models, strategies and investment decisions, but a refreshed culture adds greatly to that mix and enables companies to adapt quickly.

This example about online illustrates that the new world post-Covid raises questions for almost every organisation in the world. Some will see opportunity while others will see significant challenges. Whichever way your head is going, one thing is for certain, your culture will either enable or hinder your progress. If you think you can adapt to the new world without checking your culture, you may be missing a trick. This publication, therefore, presents an opportunity for you to reflect on that and to refresh or reboot your culture.

The messages and learning here are universal and apply to any business, of any size, in any industry, regardless of where that business is in its lifecycle. And regardless too of whether you are *business to business* (B2B), *business to consumer* (B2C) or public sector.

I always say that 'while others can copy your strategy, no one can copy your culture'. Therefore, is there not a contradiction in a book about the '4 Must-have Values' to shape your culture? Is this not a cookie-cutter approach?

I don't believe it is. The secret to making these values your own is in the detail. You should interpret them appropriately for your particular business, the dynamics in your industry and the challenges you face in your market. After all, your heritage is unique, your people are individuals with their own personalities and your particular business model has evolved over time. Your collection of stories, habits, language, jokes, acronyms and processes are all your own. And it's how you adapt and apply these four values to your business that will be your secret sauce.

I should add: more and more job applicants make their choices based on a target company's values! So if you are a business that wants to attract the best talent, take note.

What if your company already has a set of values or guiding principles in place and is not likely to change them soon? Can the messages here work for you? Well, yes they will. I believe that you'll find that the points incorporated in my four values are quite universal. For example, you may have values referring to 'team-work' or 'integrity', which are not specific in my four. However, you will find examples here in 'respect' and 'accountability' that overlap with 'team-work' and 'integrity'. It's all down to how you interpret and apply them to your particular business.

And here's a thought for career individuals. You may be a leader in your company that can drive change and persuade others to adopt these four values. If so, then the messages here will help you. On the other hand, you may not yet be in that position of influence in your company. Nevertheless, if you want to grow and develop your career and become a leader of distinction, then embrace these four values anyway in your own personal toolkit. You'll get noticed very quickly and you'll become highly marketable as a candidate.

My story is written as a parable, with a fictitious organisation and characters. The challenges in this organisation, however, are real and are a hybrid of what I have experienced over the years. I want to assure you that this is not a theoretical approach. While I use fiction to protect the innocent, the application of all concepts is real. This is the model that will work for you, as it has for countless other clients of mine through the years.

The book was written during partial lockdown due to the Covid-19 pandemic. Take a leap with me and assume that all social distancing measures were taken.

The story is set on the River Shannon in Ireland, where I have had some great and memorable trips with lots of 'craic agus ceol'. Just so you know, that's Irish (Gaelic) for 'fun and music'. All geographical locations, towns, villages and businesses are real. So too are the historical narratives. The trip starts in Carrick-on-Shannon which is on the border of Counties Leitrim and Roscommon. That's at the upper end of the River Shannon. We then go south as far as Banagher in County Offaly taking in all of the amazing sights along the way.

I could just as easily have chosen the northern route where in recent years amazing new developments and attractions have sprung up. They are a must-see for any visitor. The Acres Lake Boardwalk Trail and the Lough Key Forest Park with all sorts of adventure pursuits would keep any family occupied. But The Shed Distillery in Drumshanbo, with its medieval copper pot stills making Gunpowder Irish Gin, would have been far too much of a distraction. The characters might never have made it to the last chapter!

I'm an avid fan of Lee Child's novels. I have read every one and I love his Jack Reacher character. While I know he spends a lot of time making mincemeat of bad guys, he is highly impressive as the hero that has it all. He knows how to handle himself with guns, girls and gurriers!

The central character in my parable is Don Strudwick, a fictional character that I've had in my head for almost ten years. He is modelled on four great mentors and leaders who inspired me in my career, having worked with each one of them intensively over the years. Strudwick is an enhanced anagram of their surnames.

I was always keen to bring Don to life in some form of writing. And I promise, unlike Jack Reacher, he doesn't kill anybody. Just to be crystal clear, despite the surname, my Don Strudwick in this story is as Irish as can be. He has green blood running through his veins!

And then, just by chance …

I'm deeply interested in Irish and world history. On a recent reflective visit to Flanders, I visited several cemeteries and memorials of the Great War, from both sides of the conflict. At the end of an emotional day, I came across the grave of a very brave fifteen-year-old boy who died in 1916 as a soldier of the British Army. Believe it or not, his name was 'V.J. Strudwick'.

I know nothing of him or his family, but I'd like to think that if he had been given the chance, he might have had a great life and career. Call it fate or just serendipity, but perhaps my 'Don Strudwick' was meant to be born.

Alan O'Neill
Autumn 2020
Alanoneill.biz

1

BACK STORY

HEADING TO THE WEST OF IRELAND

Once he got past the Leixlip slip-way and left the heavy traffic behind him, the drive on the M4 became more pleasant. Heading west into the blinding sun was a challenge. It was 5.30 p.m. on a beautiful evening in July. Don Strudwick was heading to his boat which was moored in Carrick-on-Shannon in the West of Ireland. Carrick-on-Shannon is a town sitting on a series of bends in the River Shannon, the longest river in Ireland and Great Britain. His schedule had been quite hectic lately with lots of international travel and he was looking forward to the quiet two-hour drive.

Born in an urban part of Dublin, Don had spent many childhood summers on a farm with his siblings and cousins. With an abiding love for the countryside, he savoured the fragrance of the cut-grass coming in through the air vent and the vista of rolling hills ahead of him with cattle and sheep grazing without a care in the world. Watching the animals moving slowly against the backdrop of forty shades of green was just the relaxation he needed. He had an intense few days ahead of him and was glad of this short time alone. It was just perfect – nature at its best and the way it should be in this part of the world.

Don is a change management consultant and works with all sorts of organisations across the spectrum of industry. For many years, he has been supporting organisations around the world to improve their performance. But this support can be a challenge for some. That is entirely understandable,

1

particularly for owners of family businesses that have enjoyed success in the past. Sometimes business leaders can get quite entrenched in their way of doing things. They can be defensive and opinionated about their own business. So delivering hard messages is not easy. It's tough love really.

In his years of working, Don had held senior executive positions in many industries. He had achieved great success and had, of course, made many mistakes. A great all-rounder with lots of expertise as a professional manager, he was now at a point where he could safely make sense of his experiences and was happy to share them with others. He was a commercial animal and loved the intricacies of how the constituent parts of a business all knitted together. Or didn't. Despite the 'big picture' thinking, Don had a knack for deconstructing complex issues and making them simple and practical for all to understand.

GREAT TASTE DISTRIBUTORS – GTD

One of Don's current UK based clients was going through a difficult time. Great Taste Distributors (GTD) is a 50-year-old successful business that has been enjoying good growth for most of that time. Founded by John Drinkwater in 1971, it grew to be a formidable wholesaler in the Midlands. John's son James and his wife Clare took over the business in 1999 when John passed away. The business continued to grow for almost twenty more years, adding new products and new customers to its portfolio. It also added a bakery to the mix.

GTD is now a manufacturer of bakery products and a distributor of general foodstuff to hotels, restaurants, clubs and pubs around the midlands of England. Based in Leicester, it provides a weekly delivery service to its customers of catering pack foodstuffs and beverages. The current workforce of 190 is made up of a field-based sales team, a contact-centre for order-processing, a marketing team, finance and IT, procurement, a bakery, warehousing and transport, and a product team. In addition to its own bakery, GTD purchases the big-brand products from local corporates and it also imports some less well-known products from mainland Europe.

With a proud family tradition, James and Clare are very hands-on in the business. James is the Chief Executive Officer and Clare is the Finance Director. They have a son and daughter who are both in their early thirties. Sarah is married with two small children, living and working in Birmingham. She did work in sales in GTD up to the time she married, but much to James' disappointment, she left the business when she and her husband moved to Birmingham.

Tom is single and is the Purchasing Manager for GTD. After a massive row with his father, he stormed out and has been on sabbatical for the last four months. This has obviously caused a lot of tension in the family.

Sarah is now working in what James believes to be a mundane job, with no obvious career prospects. She works in sales for a Birmingham-based company. Why she won't do that for GTD is another reason for him to be disgruntled. This is the cause of endless testy debates between James and Clare. Secretly, Clare is delighted that Sarah is doing her own thing.

The financial results for 2018 and 2019 showed an unpleasant picture. While the business did make a profit, some key performance indicators were off target. Sales and margin had slipped, and cash flow was very tight for the first time since the global financial crisis in 2009. The lockdown due to the Covid-19 pandemic was an added challenge to what was a solid foundation. The business was now coming under pressure.

James and Clare are of an age where they have to start thinking about the future of the business. Both in their mid-fifties, they see themselves as having perhaps five more good years to put in, before they exit. Regardless of whether they sell the business or pass it on to their children, they know that they will have to make some changes. With numbers sliding, they know they need to get it back on track whatever their own personal plans. But it's hard to see the wood for the trees sometimes when you are so engrossed in the day to day operations.

Just before Easter, Clare convinced James to engage Don to come and take a look at the business. After much cajoling between them, Don was brought in by the pair to help them get their business back on track. Don had since completed the *discovery* phase of the project and now had a really good overview of the business. With lots to say and lots to do, he invited James and Clare to come to Ireland for a few days. Their business had been manic during the lockdown so they decided to ease their stress for a few days and join Don on the River Shannon.

ROOSKY TO CARRICK-ON-SHANNON

Leaving the M4 and sliding on to the N5, Don continued his journey, passing through the sleepy villages and towns of Bunbrosna, Multyfarnham, Rathowen and bypassing Edgeworthstown and Longford. Always curious, he tried to figure out the meaning of the names and imagined the history associated with each one. 'Ráth' was Irish for fort but he wondered what the 'Owen' in Rathowen signified. He puzzled over the meaning of Edgeworthstown. All place names in Ireland are bi-lingual and the Irish version in this case was in no way a direct translation of the anglicised version. One to Google at some other time, he thought.

Having passed through Newtownforbes he was feeling quite hungry so decided to stop for dinner. He left the N5 and pulled in to the village of Roosky – which got its name from the Irish word 'ruscaigh', meaning a marshy bog. He smiled and wondered why the early English would anglicise an Irish word and make it sound like a Russian vodka!

The sun was still shining when he finished his meal, so he went for a short walk along the banks of the River Shannon. He crossed over the eight-bar iron gate and strolled through the tree-lined avenue towards Roosky Lock. He thought some more about the feedback he would have to give to James and Clare.

His mind jumped around while he walked and he thought about the days ahead. He pondered on the foodservice industry and what he knew about it. He thought about good and bad organisations that he had worked with. He reflected on the basic things in a business-to-business distribution entity that can create a big impact. And he thought about GTD and the insights he had accumulated from his discovery process.

Not only that, Don knew that he should deliver his feedback with sensitivity. Much of what he had discovered would be a revelation for James, and probably even controversial. He would inevitably get irritated and defensive. This kind of feedback is normally presented in a boardroom with slides and fast debate. But on this occasion, Don decided on a different approach. He planned for it to be slow, calm and memorable.

He decided that he would start by setting the scene with context, to ensure that his guests accepted the need for change, in the first instance. After all, if they didn't appreciate that there was a 'burning platform', then why should they change? So he decided to give them just enough feedback and insights to challenge their thinking. Too much detail on this trip would risk them losing the bigger picture. As far as Don was concerned, a 'culture refresh' programme was needed more than anything else. Once they embraced that concept, other operational or structural changes would fall into place more easily.

He sat at the river bank and as the format for the next few days took shape in his mind and the key messages slotted into place, something caught his eye. He was distracted by movement in the water. A moving circle, ever increasing and then fading. It happened again a little to his right and this time he caught sight of a fish as it disappeared back under the flowing water.

He allowed his mind to wander from the task at hand and the days ahead. The disappearing fish reminded him of that ancient Irish folklore story of Fionn MacCumhaill and the Salmon of Knowledge. He reflected on the fable:

In ancient Ireland, Fionn Mac Cumhaill was the great leader of the Fianna. As a young boy he was sent to live with and learn from a very wise man named Finnegas. The druids often talked about a particular salmon in the River Boyne. Because it fed on golden hazelnuts from an overhanging tree, it would bring endless knowledge to the first person who ate it. For many years, Finnegas fished daily in the river to try to catch the Salmon of Knowledge so that he would forever be the wisest man in Ireland.

Having eventually caught the salmon, he instructed the young Fionn to cook it but warned him not to eat it. When he returned from a short snooze, he noticed that Fionn had bright red cheeks, full lips and beaming eyes. Finnegas asked 'have you eaten the salmon?'

'No!' Fionn replied. But he did admit that when cooking the fish on the spit, he had burned his finger and put his finger in his mouth to ease the pain. This inadvertently made him the first person to eat the Salmon of Knowledge. And so it was that Fionn became the greatest scholar and warrior in Ireland.

Don smiled to himself as he thought that perhaps Finnegas was actually a bit of a gobshite! Nevertheless, the ancient story gave him a fun idea with metaphors and analogies for the days ahead with his two guests. Don really liked James and Clare and quite enjoyed the banter between James and himself. James is a proud Englishman and loves to taunt Don with stories of English politics and sporting successes.

And so a plan fell into place. He returned to his car and continued on his journey towards Carrick-on-Shannon. He knew that the days ahead would be challenging so he planned a route on the river that would move at a slow but steady pace.

Having stopped at a shop along the way, Don reached Carrick-on-Shannon marina soon after. He unloaded the contents of the car onto the boat, put the food away, chilled the wine, brushed off the cobwebs, cleaned and opened the windows to air the cabin and started up the engines to warm them. And so he settled in on the open deck with the Raybans perched on his nose, the sun beaming on his brow, his discovery report on his lap and a nicely chilled glass of Chardonnay in his hand.

2

DISCOVERY FEEDBACK

Carrick-on-Shannon to Lough Boderg on the River Shannon

James and Clare arrived mid-morning the next day and got themselves sorted quite quickly. Having welcomed them and shown them the ropes, Don pushed off and piloted the boat out of the marina. They cruised slowly in a southerly direction under the old steel railway bridge and into Lough Tap, through the peaceful canal at picturesque Albert Lock and into Lough Boderg. James and Clare gave Don an update on business performance in recent weeks and seemed to be relaxing in to the mood of the river.

Don pointed out some rugged old stone ruins on the river banks, telling short stories of famine times. Clare listened and spotted a grey heron sitting on a dead tree stump protruding out of the water's edge. She searched for its partner and spotted it wading in the shallower water near the bank.

After a couple of hours of cruising, chatting, laughing and sightseeing, they all felt peckish. Don steered towards the west bank of Lough Boderg into a quiet cove and pulled back on the throttles. With only a gentle current and no wind, the boat came to a virtual stop. Without saying a word, he walked to the bow of the boat, unhooked the anchor, returned to the pilot seat and pressed a button on the dashboard. With the clinking rhythmic sound of a chain the anchor slowly descended. He poured some wine and waited. In a very deliberate fashion, he wanted his guests to truly unwind. He had some strong messages for them that would require a certain mood.

The boat was facing in a southerly direction. The gentle southerly current caused it to drift forward until the anchor caught hold of something solid on the river surface. With the bow of the boat locked in position, the stern swung slowly around like an arc until the bow was then facing north. Don reversed the engines just a little to test the strength of the anchor lock. The boat didn't move and Don was satisfied that the boat was secure. His slow movements helped to create the right atmosphere and help his guests to unwind.

Over a light lunch, James enquired about Don's observations from the discovery process that he had just completed. To start with and to set context, Don just summarised the process that he had used. The detail of his findings would come later. He knew that he'd have to deliver the messages carefully and in digestible chunks. He had already met with James and Clare on several occasions throughout the discovery and knew their individual styles by now. He was also very aware of the family tension beneath the surface.

James was a volatile character with little or no patience. He was also quite set in his ways. 'After all, if it worked for my father, it'll work for us too!', was his favourite saying. He hadn't completely bought into having Don involved but was slowly coming to terms with it. Clare was much more considered in her views and was willing to listen and to make changes as needed. She was feeling the pressure at home. James and the kids were regularly at logger-heads and that culminated in the bust-up with Tom. She too was worried about the recent slide in the financial results.

Don reminded them that the discovery process started with an internal review and included meeting and chatting with several members of the GTD team. Don had met with each of the senior leaders one-to-one and several other frontline colleagues. He had also spent time in the warehouse. He reminded the pair that he had gone on field visits with two of the sales team and had accompanied a driver on his truck with deliveries. The outcome of those meetings helped to tailor an internal Workbly Employee Survey. That combination of quantitative and qualitative research would add greatly to the findings and Don's insights.

Don added that his process also included a similar study externally. He himself had visited several of their customers on his own, to listen to their feedback about GTD. This helped to populate a tailored survey which was administered and it added significantly to the feedback. After all, anecdotal feedback from meetings can be dismissed as a fallacy of informal logic. Data sets from a quantitative survey will always appease sceptics like James. James is a numbers guy, and Don knew that the data would be an essential ingredient in the mix to prove the emerging issues.

Although James and Clare had approved all stages of the process, Don noticed their level of discomfort rising. Even though they invited Don to help out, it's still not easy knowing that an external person may know some things about you that you don't know yourself.

James commented with a nervous laugh, 'I feel the same way I did when I went back to the hospital for my angiogram results.'

Don assured them that there was nothing that he found that wasn't fixable and reminded them that he would reveal all in due course. To further set the scene, he asked them both how they felt about the decline in sales and margin. James tried at first to make it seem like a temporary blip and that everything would be fine in time. But with gentle prodding from Clare, he acknowledged the recent tough meeting with their accountant and another with the bank, who had both raised concerns about profitability, cash-flow and their new reality. With reluctant acceptance, James acknowledged that indeed things would have to change.

Don posed the questions, 'What are your personal plans for the future? In other words, when would you both like to retire and slow down a bit?'

Clare immediately answered, 'As we've said before, I think we should be thinking about a five-year window, as there is so much that I'd like to do. We haven't had a decent holiday in years and we don't have enough time for our grandchildren either.'

James interjected, 'Well I won't be going anywhere with the way things are. And now after this coronavirus scare, who knows what will happen?'

'Leaving aside the timeframe for now, what is your preference? Is it to sell the business or to pass it on to the kids?' asked Don.

James frowned, 'I would have liked for Tom and Sarah to take it over, after all that's what I did! But it's unlikely to happen now.'

Clare suggested that 'Selling it is probably the better solution, as I don't want Tom and Sarah to have an albatross around their necks.'

James sulked and snapped back at Clare, 'It's not an albatross! It's a damn good business and it's profitable. They just need to cop on to themselves!'

Don didn't react but reminded them that whichever route they take, getting the business back on track was essential. If they want to get the value from selling the asset, then sales and profitability would need to return to what they were before. 'Likewise,' he said, 'if your kids were to come back in, I'm sure you wouldn't want them to be fighting against the tide from the start.'

Don used this approach to focus them on an end-goal. This, he thought, was essential as it would help James and Clare to put all the feedback that they were about to hear in context. Otherwise, why should they embrace change?

After a short silence, James started to come round to accepting the reality of the situation. Moving the conversation along, they discussed the financial results some more. James offered some reasons for the sales decline. 'The sales team need to get more fire in their belly. They're making it easy for the competitors to sneak in the back door,' he said. He went on to add that the reason for the margin decline is the crazy discounting that's going on in the industry. 'It's all about price' he said. 'Customers have no loyalty anymore, after all we've done for them over the years. One hotel in particular switched to a competitor for 35p per tray of bottled waters,' he added.

Clare agreed with some of that sentiment but in a less forceful way than James. She said, to no one in particular, 'I sometimes wonder are we giving our customers what they really need or are we simply doing what we've always done?'

After some further discussion, Don asked both of his guests to consider a question. 'Disney executives believe there is one prominent driver of success in their business. What do you think it is?' he asked.

As they started to answer, Don interrupted, raised his right index finger in the air, paused and then excused himself and said 'Give me fifteen minutes. I'm going for a power-nap,' and was snoring within minutes.

Clare and James looked at each other with astonishment but said nothing. They had met Don a number of times and had come to terms with his occasional oddness. They sat back on the open deck and debated his question. They both uttered a few of the obvious answers such as high occupancy rate, great food, professional people, fabulous theme parks, clean bedrooms, interesting location, leisure and spa facilities, fun atmosphere, top class service and so on. But after some time they speculated that Don had more than likely asked a question where the answer was probably a bit less obvious than that.

Don returned and listened to the closing debate. He said, 'While Disney's results are indeed spectacular, they believe that the biggest driver of success for them is customer retention. They have metrics that show that approximately 70 percent of visitors return again. This is despite the fact that customers' credit cards melt as they spend their way through the park.'

James added, 'So if guest retention is a key driver, then guest satisfaction in the first place must be the secret.'

After a minute of silence Clare interjected, 'But isn't that so blatantly obvious? Everyone knows that, so am I missing something?'

'Yes, but isn't it cool when a corporation as big as Disney with sales of approximately $70 billion and earnings of $11 billion actually shout it from the rooftops?' said Don, as Clare nodded in agreement. 'And if it was so obvious then why doesn't every business just do it?' he added. 'Not only that, it's the way that guest satisfaction is such a priority in every aspect of their business. They live and breathe it every single day. It's inherent in their culture.'

'I have no doubt that Disney measures everything to within an inch of its life,' said James, 'so I guess they mean it.'

Don started the engines, released the anchor and headed slowly in a southerly direction as he added, 'customer satisfaction is a concept however that should apply to any business, big or small. So let's see if we can bring the message to life for GTD when we stop later for dinner. Roosky Bridge up ahead is too low for our boat so we'll have to call ahead to have the bridge lifted. When we get through that and then through the lock on the other side, we'll be on our merry way to Tarmonbarry, where we are staying tonight.'

Don went on to add, 'Obviously for Disney, it's because of the experience that guests have while they are there.' He shared his view of the importance of customer experience. 'There was a time when organisations could differentiate themselves with a great product, or so they thought. But with globalisation and the ease of buying products from almost any country in the world online that is less likely now. In your local convenience store for example, its range of products is almost a mirror image of its competitor's collection in the store further down the street.'

He continued, 'Banks have even recognised this. Retail banks used to advertise their mortgage products mainly on rate, but now they too recognise the need to offer other advantages. And this concept of "customer-first" is not just a priority for business-to-consumer (B2C) companies like those in the retail or hospitality sectors. Business-to-business (B2B) companies like yours also need to recognise this new reality.'

As they rounded the bend facing Dromod Harbour, their conversation was interrupted by James' telephone ringing. Recognising the number, he excused himself and took the call. Returning ten minutes later, he described the call. One of his Italian suppliers had just informed him of an increase in pricing which he had been resisting for the past week. But when they assured him that GTD would be their sole UK importer going forward, he accepted the increase.

This story enabled the conversation to develop and James began to eat his previous words, accepting that customers do make judgements based on a set of criteria, and not just price.

Within minutes, Don stopped the boat at a concrete platform erected in the centre of the river, just yards from Roosky Bridge. He telephoned the lock-keeper to have the bridge raised. While waiting, Don opened a bag, took out some rice paper, edible ink and a bag of hazelnuts. He wrote the words:

'Customer satisfaction is a key driver of long-term business results.'

He scrunched the rice paper around the hazelnut and threw it into the water, without saying a word.

James and Clare were now coming to terms with Don's cryptic style and sense of humour and decided not to say a word either. They knew that all would be revealed in good time. Don started up the engine again, advanced slowly under the raised bridge and within minutes they were approaching Roosky Lock.

ROOSKY TO TARMONBARRY

After greeting the lock-keeper in person and entering Roosky Lock, the trio waited for the water level to drop. James was stationed at the bow, holding the rope, and got talking to the occupants of the boat in front. He chatted with a group of German anglers who had hired a cruiser for the week. They had a quantity of fishing rods and other angling equipment on deck that suggested they were going to empty the Shannon of all and sundry.

Don stayed at the helm while Clare held the rope at the stern. As Don and Clare chatted with the lock-keeper, James was laughing and joking with his new acquaintances.

A few minutes after exiting the lock, the river widened into Lough Forbes. Don told them the story of the Forbes family from Aberdeen being gifted the estate by the British Crown in 1691. 'The great fire of 1825 would have brought total havoc to the castle in 1825, if it wasn't for Pilot their dog. Pilot's barking was enough to waken and save the occupants,' said Don.

'There'll be even louder barking from me if you don't come on and tell me the findings from your discovery,' said James with a laugh.

Don was sensitive to James' sense of pride and started to point out lots of good things he discovered from meeting and surveying customers of GTD. He complimented the efficient order process and the friendliness of the team in the contact centre. He continued with more examples of good customer focus from the accounts department in particular. He described the willingness of the warehouse team to accommodate a customer in distress. 'One customer was particularly impressed with the arrival of their two cases of yoghurt by taxi one Friday evening,' said Don. He watched for James' reaction to that and wasn't surprised to see a surly look on his face.

Don went on to identify some areas of concern however. It seemed that out-of-stocks was a big issue. 'The thing is,' said Don, 'once the customer places an order and someone from your team accepts it, they assume that the order will arrive.' He added 'What really upsets them is that they only find out about an item being out-of-stock when their delivery arrives.'

James interjected, 'I'll bet that's what happened with the delivery by taxi you mentioned. What you described as good service Don, had a ridiculous cost to us. I can guarantee you it's because somebody screwed up in the first place,' he said.

'Not to mention the fact that we surely lost money on that transaction,' added Clare.

Don appeased them by once again complimenting the service recovery on that occasion but he agreed with the commercial nonsense.

James argued that out-of-stocks are measured clinically and denied that it could actually be a big problem. 'After all,' he said, 'the warehouse has metrics that prove we achieve 99.1 percent delivery accuracy and that's a digital report, not a manual count.'

Clare went on to remind him that she had pointed out in the past that they were not measuring the right thing. 'As I told you before James, it's easy to hit 99.1 percent of delivery agreements when you're only counting what's in stock. But what about the out-of-stocks that the warehouse pickers put a line through before the metrics kick in? Sure it's no wonder, in that case their metrics should be 100 percent,' she said.

After some more debate, James seemed to be resisting the importance of customer service. 'That's more for restaurants and shops,' he said. 'It's not as relevant in our B2B world. As I said earlier, our customers are all about price, and that's all they care about.'

Recognising that this would be an uphill climb, Don and Clare persisted with more examples of customer service. Don turned the focus of the conversation and asked James, 'Think for a moment about your top ten suppliers. Apart from price, what are your reasons for buying from them?'

James went on to give examples of one supplier having a fantastic product range. With another example, he alluded to a terrific supply chain that guaranteed availability of core lines all year round. Another example was because of the level of trust between the two companies that has not been breached in more than 30 years of collaborating. This then paved the way for Don to remind James of the telephone call he had taken earlier in the day.

Don then revealed to James and Clare some more detail of his conversations with GTD customers. He said, 'I asked every one of your customers the same question that I asked you. I asked about what was most important to them. And I have to tell you, that not one of them mentioned price in their top three issues. In fact they even admitted to me that they'd be willing to pay a slight premium if they could be guaranteed that they'd receive what they ordered, on time every time.'

While James and Clare absorbed that golden nugget, Don went on to express his concerns about some other negative feedback. Issues that included the attitude and behaviours of some of the drivers.

'We don't do our own deliveries, we outsource that to a service provider,' said Clare. 'But, of course, as far as the customer is concerned, those drivers are GTD drivers and we never told them how we want them to behave.'

With that breakthrough comment, Don closed off the conversation with a couple of more examples regarding lack of innovation. He knew progress was being made with changes in Clare's mindset at least.

With an air of acceptance, James and Clare acknowledged that while they had a strong heritage, great team, a fantastic product range and a good customer base, that wasn't enough anymore.

'Look,' said James, 'I know business is changing dramatically. We have lots of new competitors now. The big guys are even starting to service the smaller customers. They have deeper pockets than us and there's no way we can compete on price, even if we wanted to. But what the heck can we do?'

Clare also started to look anxious and Don reassured them that there was a lot they could do to compete very effectively. Once again, he reminded them that he wanted them to first of all hear and understand the feedback, and to absorb the insights from that feedback. 'I promise you,' he said 'we will come back to all of this and address it with a detailed action plan.'

As they approached the last bend in the river before arriving at Tarmonbarry, Don reached for the rice paper, the edible ink and another hazelnut. He scribbled the words:

'Customer experience is the new battleground.'

He scrunched it up as before and tossed it into the river.

As they pulled up on the north side of Tarmonbarry Lock, Don reminded his guests that they would be staying the night in Keenan's and dining in the Purple Onion restaurant.

3

CULTURE

OVERNIGHT IN TARMONBARRY

The Royal Canal that carried passengers and freight from Tarmonbar-ry-Cloondara on the River Shannon eastwardly towards Dublin, is steeped in history. Opened in 1817 before railways arrived in Ireland, it served as an important artery for trade and transport from the west of Ireland. Life was altogether much slower in those days, with horses pulling the barges at a walking pace. As Don explained the history and painted the picture for his guests, the ever-impatient James who was chomping at the bit for more discovery insights, wondered if Don was reliving that era.

As Don tied up at the mooring and locked down the boat, he told an important story that is linked to the locality. He described the Irish famine of 1845–1849 that brought permanent change in the country's demographic, cultural and political landscape. He pointed out on a map the Irish National Famine Museum in Strokestown, which is 20 minutes west of Tarmonbarry by car. 'This is where 1,490 starving tenants of Strokestown Park were evicted and forced to walk to Dublin along the banks of the Royal Canal. From there they boarded a ship to Liverpool. They then sailed on four so-called 'coffin ships' that took them to Quebec, with over half of them perishing along the way,' said Don.

James asked Don how the Irish of today feel about the famine to which Don replied, 'It was a very different time in terms of Ireland's political status, the economy, our beliefs and our culture. To a great extent, it had a huge impact on our national culture and on our thinking to this day. After all, it wasn't that long ago. My grandparents were children of people born around that time.' Then he added, 'But that's enough about that, I'm telling you that history to illustrate the importance of and the impact of culture, but more about that later,' he said as he guided them to their accommodation.

With a smell of freshly cut grass in the air, Don and his guests made the short walk from the mooring to Keenan's, where James and Clare checked into their room. Don sat in Keenan's Gastro-Bar waiting for his guests to return. Soon after, the trio settled in taking stock of their surroundings, while Don ordered Guinness for everyone.

As they savoured the first taste of the stout, Don said 'I'd like to share some of the high-level findings from the Workbly internal employee survey and my various one-to-one meetings, if that's okay with you?'

'Firstly,' he asked, 'what scores do you yourselves expect in the survey?'

James was first to respond, 'Well, obviously what I'd like to hear is different to what I'm going to hear. I'm hoping for high scores but after what you told us about our customer feedback, I'll hold my breath, if you don't mind!'

Clare as usual, was tuned in and candidly said she expected to do well in some of the "operations" type questions but not so well in "culture" type questions.

With that mix, Don knew that he needed to be careful. Whatever their customers think is one thing, but because this is a family business, he knew that negative feedback would be hard for the Drinkwaters to take.

Don started by giving the scores for the quantitative Workbly survey.

'Clare is right,' he started 'you have done well in the "operations" category and also the section on "wellbeing". It seems to me that you are being quite caring and possibly parental in your management style.'

James jumped in, 'It's probably because we pay them too much, if you ask me'.

'It's comforting to see that your "engagement" scores are good and that gives us a lot to build on,' said Don. 'The "leadership" and "culture" categories are both causing some challenges for you,' he added. 'But look, the numbers are only a starting point, the real gold dust is in the anecdotal feedback that I have for you,' said Don. 'The comments will help you to understand the numbers.'

'How does all of that come together?' asked James.

Don replied by explaining that his comments and insights from hereon are based on the scores in the survey, the comments that employees typed into the survey and also from Don's own one-to-one meetings with various colleagues.

Don guided James and Clare into the Purple Onion restaurant next door for dinner. They settled in after being greeted by owners Pauline and Paul Dempsey. Over starters, Don again reminded his guests of the people that he had met in the discovery. He had interviewed all senior leaders. He went out on customer field visits with two different salespeople and also accompanied a van driver with deliveries.

James listened intently as he ate his warm spicy prawns. Clare enjoyed her super-food salad with hummus as Don spoke between bites of "Ummera Smokehouse" chicken. He started by pointing out the great successes that the company had enjoyed to date. He gave some more positive feedback on the general product range, the spread of customers, the modern bakery and distribution centre and the sophisticated IT system.

'The business model is very strong and, generally speaking, it works very well,' said Don.

'You have a high volume of transactions each day, at low to medium sales value. All that makes everybody very busy indeed. Consequently, because everyone is so busy doing the day-job, I think some of your team may be missing the opportunity to stand back and see the big picture sometimes.'

Clare interrupted, 'Because everyone is so busy Don, it may be hiding the fact that we always seem to be firefighting.'

'But we have an operations meeting every Monday and a monthly management meeting,' said James. 'Why don't these issues get raised then?' he asked.

'Look,' said Don, 'we'll get to all that detail in time but nobody is denying that meetings take place, it's more about the style of the meetings. And that relates to the culture of your organisation.'

Whether it was the Guinness or the Malbec is not clear, or the general ambience and peaceful nature of the trip, but James reacted this time with calmness. By now he was seeing a pattern emerge that he could either choose to resist and be defensive towards, or he could recognise that he was now sitting with two people who genuinely cared about helping him and the business.

But that still doesn't mean they're right, he thought to himself.

The conversation was interrupted with the arrival of the main course. Clare smiled at the beautifully dressed pan-fried fillets of sea bass, while James delighted at his seared Thornhill duck breast. Don settled in to his forest mushroom and blue-cheese risotto. After some brief chat with the friendly waitress, they discussed the great service and the food for a few minutes as they each identified their favourite national cuisine. James' passion was for oriental dishes while Clare and Don shared their preference for Italian cuisine.

'What's all this stuff about culture?' said James with a smirk and a hint of sarcasm. 'Is this not just some psychobabble that consultants like to go on about?'

Don didn't quite take the bait directly but instead he asked James what it was about oriental dishes that he preferred.

'It's probably a combination of the spices and the sauces they use,' he said.

He then went on to describe a recent vacation where he and Clare had visited Thailand and Vietnam. 'We actually had a Thai cookery lesson in our hotel in Phuket and another in Ho Chi Minh City. While there are obvious similarities such as rice, noodles and both being almost dairy-free, there are subtle differences.'

'Yes,' added Clare, 'the Vietnamese food is quite light but you can see the French influence in the way they include potatoes and baguettes.'

James and Clare continued with some more stories about their holiday. They chatted about the differences in the people in both countries, the architecture, dress code, language and more. As Don took a rest from his food, he said with a smile, 'Now that's culture! Every country has its own distinct culture that makes them clearly identifiable and differentiates them from other countries. That might be to do with language, religion, dress code, ways of greeting, the bone structure and skin type of the locals, even the traffic on the roads,' he added. 'James, you are a well-travelled man, if you were teleported to any country in the world without being told in advance, do you think that you'd know where you are?'

'I think I probably would,' replied James. 'Even if that included Tarmon-barry,' he giggled. 'Look around you, I can see that most people here are Irish. I can also tell you that the group of four men in the corner are German,' he added.

Now highly impressed, Don quizzed him on how he knew that.

'Well there are two reasons, firstly they're all drinking Guinness and despite the reputation that the Irish have, I know they are probably not likely to be doing that over dinner,' he said, then paused. 'And okay, the second reason is that they introduced themselves to me in Roosky Lock,' as he laughed heartily at his own wit.

Don was delighted that James was a little more relaxed.

'Each country's own culture has built up over time,' Don continued.

'I know we shouldn't generalise but there are some obvious norms that are backed up by data, that illustrate culture traits. Leaving aside the examples we already mentioned, like language and food, you can even see national cultural norms in economics. Ireland is traditionally known for exporting beer and butter, although that has changed with the growth of the pharmaceutical, technology and life-sciences sectors in recent years. Italy on the other hand is known for its fashion, wine and olive oil. Germany's reputation is built on its heavy industries such as motor cars.'

'What about in the workplace?' asked Clare.

'Well, I find culture in the workplace quite fascinating,' said Don. 'There are very distinct differences around the world in terms of how decisions are made, or how people communicate in the workplace. Take an obvious one as an example. In Far Eastern cultures, decisions are often deferred to the leaders and hierarchy is very important to them. That's cultural.'

'So is it mainly to do with East and West?' asked James.

'Not necessarily,' answered Don. 'You will even see differences across Europe. And some of that goes back hundreds of years to national heritage. Southern Europe was heavily influenced by Roman culture, in other words, it's quite authoritarian. Northern European countries on the other hand are less so, probably due to the strong egalitarian Viking influence.'

'Actually, that reminds me,' said Clare. 'Remember the difficulties we had with that new IT guy that arrived to us from Netherlands? He really struggled with the way we speak to one another.' She added, 'the Dutch like to think they are very straight, but some of his colleagues were often offended with some of his comments.'

'That's a great example,' said Don. 'In the same way that every country has its own distinct culture, every single organisation in the world also has its own culture,' Don continued. 'Some are quite advanced and have designed the culture that they believe will enable them to win. Most others however have not and I believe they're missing a trick,' he added.

'But how do you define culture?' asked Clare. 'While I know there is a lot written about it and I know it's important, what does it mean in an organisation?'

Don replied, 'It's commonly defined as "the way we do things around here". That refers to a combination of behaviours, such as what people do and the way that they do it, and what people say and the way they say it. It's also often described as the "software of the mind". The phone in your pocket has an operating system. It doesn't matter whether it's android or an iPhone.

Can you imagine how effective that device would be without its operating system?'

As James took out his phone, Don quickly added 'Let me give you an example: James, how would you describe the culture in the Italian company that called you earlier?'

'Bloody expensive,' laughed James, putting the phone back in his pocket. 'But seriously, I suppose they are very customer-focused and good communicators,' he added. 'But they were all nice as pie on the one hand so they could tell me about a price increase,' he grunted.

'Yes,' said Clare, 'but they did call you. Price increases are a reality and they have to make a profit after all, but that call is just typical of the way they always work with us. They're honest and always proactive.'

'Precisely,' said Don.

'Culture is not just about the fluffy stuff. There is no contradiction between being customer-focused and making money.'

Clare went on to share an experience she had with their auditors. 'During the Covid lockdown, they were so proactive. They contacted us very early at the start of the lockdown to check if we were fully aware of the new regulations and payment schemes. That really impressed me and made me feel we were in safe hands,' she said. 'And I'd say this restaurant has a good customer-focused culture. The service is excellent. So it proves that it's relevant for any size company.'

'Culture also shows itself in the way that internal meetings are held, how decisions are made, how people speak to each other, how people take responsibility, or they don't!' said Don.

'I'll bet right now that you would recognise a silo culture where departments don't interact effectively with each other. And I'll bet you'd also recognise a blame culture in an organisation, wouldn't you?' asked Don.

'I hate to admit it James, but I can recognise both of those traits in our company,' said Clare.

'I wasn't necessarily referring to GTD with that comment,' said Don. 'It's just that these traits are so common yet they are very destructive,' he added. 'Especially with the challenges of a post-Covid world, organisations have to think more about productivity on the one hand and attractiveness as an employer on the other.'

Although he noticed that James looked a little deflated, Don didn't backtrack. This conversation was so essential and James needed to appreciate both the importance of the challenge and the urgency of it. Nevertheless, he didn't want James or Clare to think that their organisation was unique in not having a defined culture.

'Because culture permeates every strand of a business, I'm regularly surprised at how all of this gets missed. And even some of the big corporates that claim to have a defined culture, are not living it,' he added. To me it's all about consistency. Just like a great orchestra has a strong rhythm for every tune they play, a company culture can also bring that consistency,' he added. 'Can you imagine the awful sound of a bad trumpeter in an orchestra and how grating it would be? While a bad musician clearly stands out in an orchestra, negative traits in culture are not always so obvious. But for sure the impact will be felt in places.'

'Am I right in saying that culture eats strategy for breakfast?' asked James proudly.

Impressed and smiling, 'That's right' said Don. 'In fact I'm a firm believer in that narrative as I have seen it first-hand so many times in my work.'

'Yes, well let's make sure that it doesn't eat our dessert!' said James. 'Come on, who's going to join me?' he giggled while quite delighted with another example of his own wit.

'Guys, this is the kernel of what GTD needs to focus on. The detailed feedback that we'll discuss over the next couple of days all comes back to one thing, and that's culture,' said Don. 'If you get this right, you can take on the world. And if you really get this right, I promise that you will be able to shape your organisation and get it back on track. And think about that, when we get it back on track the value will grow again,' he added.

Clare was quiet for a bit and then added 'I wonder will that encourage the kids to get back involved?'

'Well let's park that for now,' said James awkwardly. 'We'll get to that but for now, I'm still not convinced about this culture lark. Don, if it's so important how does a company go about creating a culture that's unique to them?'

'You've just hit the nail on the head,' said Don. 'Your culture should be tailored for you. It has to pay respect to your heritage, your ambition, the industry you're in and what's important to you. In fact, I firmly believe that a great culture is so distinctive that nobody else can copy it. Your competitors may well copy your strategy, your product range, your marketing ideas and even your website layout. But they cannot copy how your teams behave, how they work together or how they build rapport with your customers. That'll be your secret recipe.'

As the table was cleared, they complimented the service and popped back into Keenan's Bar for a nightcap.

'I'm curious,' said James 'what's involved in shaping our culture? If this is going to be a big deal, I'm just not sure,' he said.

'Well James, I'm beginning to realise that we can't afford not to do it,' replied Clare. 'And let's bear in mind that the company culture we have right now has been built up over many years, both in your parents' time and now in ours. We can't expect this to be a quick fix.'

Don acknowledged Clare's point but also reassured them that this is all very possible. 'You're not the first company in the world to go through a culture refresh,' he added. 'There is a methodology and it's built on having an agreed set of values or guiding principles.'

James didn't look convinced.

'Each of us lives our personal lives by a set of values. Undoubtedly, we care about the world and other people, we're respectful, honest and trustworthy,' said Don. 'Now, let's just take respect as an example.'

As James averted his eyes and looked down at the table, Don continued.

'James, I want you to imagine you were sitting on a packed train, there are many others standing as there are no more available seats. What would you do if a pregnant girl or an elderly gent boarded at the next stop?'

Without saying a word and smirking, James looked at the others.

'Don't you dare,' said Clare as she fondly slapped the back of his hand.

'Well of course, I'd give up my seat,' he said.

'Yes you would,' said Don, 'because you have respect for others. You were taught about respect as a child and your parents instilled it in you. And now, whenever you are presented with a situation that demands your respect, you automatically respond accordingly with appropriate behaviours, actions or words,' he said. 'And this is where modern progressive organisations nail it. When they agree their own set of values or guiding principles, communicate them and measure their people against these values, that's when they get breakthrough.'

'Yes but does that mean we have to have all of those silly words hanging on the wall of our reception, such as integrity, teams, etc?' asked James cynically.

'Of course not,' answered Don 'but we will identify a set that are right for you and make sure that they become embedded in a measurable way. And don't forget we already have had a steer on what values need to be prioritised from the Workbly employee engagement survey. Remember, we asked your people for their views,' he said.

'What I particularly like about that approach,' said Clare 'is that we asked everybody. As a result, their level of engagement with the new culture will surely increase,' she added.

'That's absolutely correct,' said Don. 'And over the next couple of days we'll develop a draft set that we can then take back in order to show everybody that you've listened to them and taken their input seriously.'

Over in the far corner, a group of musicians started playing traditional Irish music. The fiddle, the guitar, the flute and the accordion played tunes that drowned out any possibility of further chat. The Germans had also relocated to Keenan's and the sound levels went up some more.

'Now,' said Don, 'this is more of our Irish culture. Let's forget about work. It's time for some "craic agus ceol,"' as he ordered a second round of night-caps.

'Craic?' asked James. 'Don't worry, it's not what you think,' said Don.

Back at the boat, Don reflected on the day and what he had shared so far. He knew that James in particular would be impatient and want both the feedback and actions agreed quickly. But Don reminded himself that if they moved to action-planning too quickly, then Don would not absorb the seriousness of the messages. He knew that his pace was frustrating James, but remained convinced that he was doing the right thing.

For this trip, he wanted to build context with the big picture first, by positioning the importance of culture. He planned to leave the detailed planning for the leadership two-day workshop due to happen in Leicester in a couple of weeks.

Before turning off his cabin light, Don wrote another message on rice paper, wrapped it around a hazelnut and threw it into the water.

'Organisational culture is often defined as "the way we do things around here", including actions, behaviours and words.'

4

CUSTOMER-CENTRICITY

TARMONBARRY TO LANESBOROUGH

Don was awakened early the next morning by the guttural animal-like sound of a cormorant. It was the only sound in an otherwise peaceful and idyllic setting. The bird was perched on top of a red river marker. Don reflected on the previous evening. He was getting the measure of James' style and wit and was growing to like him even more, seeing him in this different environment.

But he also knew that he still had work to do in convincing him of the need to change. Clare was an ally from the start and he knew he could use that if he had to. But knowing what he did about the recent family tension, he didn't want to add to that and cause a further rift. Don was more determined to shift James' mindset through logic and good debate. But knowing that logic is not always persuasive when pride and other emotions are in the way, he also considered other tactics.

Over breakfast, James and Clare chatted about the discussion from the previous night.

'I'm not convinced about this culture stuff Clare,' said James. 'It all sounds a bit fluffy to me and I think we've enough to be doing now to get the business back on track. I really thought that we'd be discussing strategy and pricing and whatever else.'

Clare interjected quite firmly, 'James, we have to give this a chance. We're here for a couple of days and let's not jump to conclusions yet. I've no doubt that Don knows what he's doing and we'll both have to trust him for now.'

They checked out of Keenan's and made their way back to the boat, where they found Don sitting on the transom wading his feet in the water. Beside him was a large glass of orange juice and his paraphernalia for recording nuggets of wisdom. He once again wrote a message on rice paper.

'Others may copy your strategy, but no one can copy your culture.'

After he wrapped it around a hazelnut and threw it in the river, Clare asked about this strange ceremony. With a smile, Don told the story of the Salmon of Knowledge and amusingly suggested that he was leaving his wisdom for another salmon to absorb and for it to pass on to the next Fionn MacCumhaill.

Don started up the engines as James untied the ropes. They approached the nearby lock and waited for it to open. As they entered the lock, James was greeted with banter once again by his new German friends. When the water level dropped to allow the lock gates to open on the south side, Don invited James to get behind the wheel and take over the piloting. As James quickly got the hang of it, he expressed his surprise at how slowly the boat reacted to the turn of the wheel. Don reminded him of how to avoid rocks by navigating between the black and red markers.

Don informed them that they would be cruising for another 40 minutes or so till they reached Lanesborough. Travelling at a very steady eight knots, Don pointed out some beautiful scenic spots to Clare and James. It was a warm day. The early sun was casting long shadows on the rolling green fields. The noise of the Volvo diesel engines was eventually forgotten as the sound of the breaking waves and wash behind the boat took over. There was a fresh smell in the air and Clare savoured the slight breeze on her face as they headed south. James was very relaxed and enjoying himself, Don noted.

The only other human contact on that stretch was when another cruiser came towards them from the south. Like duelling knights on very slow white horses, they approached each other from a distance. Then with friendly waves and smiles they passed each other on their respective port sides. James was getting into the mood of the river and seemed to be enjoying the relaxation. A perfect remedy for more key messages, thought Don.

'Clare and James,' said Don. 'I'd like to chat to you about your customers. I don't need to give you any more feedback from my discovery or examples of the issues to do with your levels of customer experience. Some of those are practical operational issues that, with the right people in the room, you'll be able to address. I suppose I'm more concerned about why these things are happening. The underlying causes and how we can prevent them going forward.'

'Yes,' said Clare. 'The market has changed beyond recognition since the Covid-19 lockdown. We're finding that we're getting more orders online now. While that's great from an efficiency and cost perspective, I'm also concerned.'

'Why is that?' asked James.

'Well, if we're seeing such a migration to online, there are two issues to consider. One is that the customers' expectations will shift with digital and the opportunities for us to influence their orders will diminish. Our technology is going to need more investment,' she added.

'Don't get me started on IT,' said James. 'We have already spent a fortune in the last couple of years and we now have a team of three in that department that we never had before. That's another ongoing fortune,' he added.

'I really don't think we have a choice in that,' said Clare. 'And don't forget that we have saved payroll due to having one less salesperson. But the other concern I have is that our competitors have deeper pockets and can invest more heavily in technology. How can we compete with that?' she added.

Don said, 'There is a new reality too that we need to keep in mind. More than 70 percent of the decision-makers in the world of B2B are millennials! They themselves are consumers in the B2C world and are experiencing amazing service levels in other parts of their life, so they bring those expectations to their own jobs.'

'Now don't you start Don,' said James. 'I'm sick and tired hearing about bloody millennials as if they are some new species dropped in from Mars. They are the entitled ones, if you ask me!'

'They do indeed get a lot of bad press,' said Don. 'But much of it is unfair in my view. The reality is that every new generation has differences to the previous ones. That's natural. But I've worked with lots of fantastic millennials,' he added. 'And remember, they are the first generation to be brought up with mobile phones and other sorts of amazing technology. So they expect to see it in their workplace.'

To lighten James' apparent old-fashioned thinking, Clare reminded him of the incident with their grandchild recently, where two-year-old Sammy was disgruntled from trying to change channels on the TV by swiping it.

'Let's explore what customer experience actually means in your business-to-business world,' said Don.

'Now hold on, Don,' said James as he pulled back on the throttle to allow a family of swans to cross the river. 'I appreciate the importance of customer experience in a hotel, a restaurant, or a shop. But really, don't you think that our customers are above all of that? They are professionals after all.'

Clare answered before Don. 'But James, we've heard enough feedback from Don on the practical operational things that our customers are not happy with. And I was even thinking over breakfast this morning about something that Don told me previously. Let's look at the lifetime value of any one of our customers. If we take a sample customer that places a weekly order with us of £1,000, that's a total of £50,000 in one year. Agreed?'

James nodded.

'Then imagine if we multiply that by say, ten more years, that's a lifetime value of over £500,000. And as we both know, ten years is nothing when you think of the long-term partnerships we have with many of our customers!' After a further pause, she added 'that's enough to convince me that we have work to do. Don't forget we're not the only company that they can buy from! And if we start slipping on our service levels, why should they stay with us?'

Don wrote on the rice paper:

'Keep in mind the lifetime potential of each customer, rather than just the value of today's transaction.'

'You're right,' said Don as he wrapped the rice paper around a hazelnut then threw it into the river. 'There is certainly a piece of work to be done here to clearly identify what level and what detail of customer experience is right for GTD. And that's not just a broad brush-stroke approach. There are certain assumptions we can make across the board,' he added. 'But at your level of volume and money, you need to treat every single customer as if they are unique. After all, you have enough information on each customer to be able to personalize your offering to suit their individual needs.'

'That's absolutely true,' said Clare. 'And they're now expecting that. For example James, we could easily tailor our promotions for key customers!'

'Alright I do accept that it makes some sense,' conceded James. 'But that sounds like a one-off exercise that the sales teams should do. But how do we make sure that it will always be top of mind? And by the way, do you know what frustrates me? There was a time that we knew each one of our customers personally and we had a great relationship with them. Now many of them have either moved on or are retired. Now we have all these young people making decisions and wanting everything online,' he added with a scowl.

'Yes,' said Clare 'but think of the age profile of most of our salespeople. I did the calculation and the average age is 49. We have to help them better understand how to connect and build rapport with all customers and of course, to embrace technology. They're dealing with a new way of working and we haven't helped them enough.'

'To start with,' added Don, 'agreeing a new way of servicing your customers is not just a task for the sales guys. I think you should include all departments in that customer-mapping exercise and get them all thinking about their role and contribution. Just like a great stage show has cast and back-stage crew and like a football team has forwards and full-backs,' he added.

'However, I do want to make a point about your salespeople,' he continued. 'Sometimes salespeople are in danger of treating regular repeat customers in a robotic uninspiring way. What I mean by that,' he quickly added 'is they tend to have a routine that focuses mainly on taking the order. They seldom take time to truly listen to their customers.'

'Wow,' said James. 'That's a big statement. Are you saying that our sales-people are useless?'

'Of course I'm not,' replied Don. 'But I am saying that from time to time, and at the very least once a season, they should have a structured chat with their customers over a coffee to see what challenges they're facing and to see how they can solve them,' he added. 'Now that will differentiate you, because in a continuity business like yours, that seldom happens.' That added some spice to the conversation and Don let it sink in for a few minutes before continuing.

'Moving on from that,' added Don, we need to consider calling out the importance of putting the customer at the heart of all decision-making. It needs to be part of the culture and we need a specific value to be named for it. How do you both feel about that?'

Clare gave her immediate assent and James said nothing.

'We can work out the wording another time, but for now, we're all agreed that you need to *put the customer at the heart of everything that you do* and front and centre in all decision-making, am I right?' asked Don.

'Yes,' said James, 'but what exactly do you mean by that? What does it entail?'

'Remember we chatted yesterday about customer experience being the new battleground? There is a real commercial benefit to taking this seriously. Clare already calculated the lifetime-value of a typical customer, and she is completely right. But it doesn't stop there. When customers get that great experience consistently, they buy more because they know that they can trust you. It's a no-brainer, honestly,' said Don.

'It's also good for morale,' added Clare. 'It's so much more motivating and satisfying when you get positive feedback, rather than getting complaints or constantly firefighting.'

'Mm, I guess so,' said James. 'And that firefighting often costs us money when trying to recover from those errors,' he added. 'That bloody taxi story is still bugging me.'

'Let's first of all consider what we mean by "great customer experience"' said Don. 'I'd like to give you a framework that will give you great help in deciding "what good looks like" at every customer touch-point. And the analogy is that of a three-legged stool.'

'Hold on a second,' laughed James. 'I know we're in rural Ireland, but you're not planning on taking us to milk cows, are you?'

'Not likely,' said Clare. I'd be worried that you mightn't know the difference between a cow and a bull!'

With a look from James that would melt Mount Everest, Don giggled and made the coffee.

While waiting for the coffee to brew, Don performed his little ritual with the rice paper.

'Put the customer at the heart of everything that you do – front and centre of all decision-making.'

LANESBOROUGH, CO. LONGFORD

James navigated the boat around a bend and the river opened up wide as they approached the town of Lanesborough. Because the current was a little slower here, Don asked James if he'd like to try mooring so they could have a relaxed coffee. With little direction from Don, James skilfully reversed the boat alongside a berth and successfully moored without a bump.

Over coffee, Don explained the rationale for the stool. 'In the same way that we made a judgement on the Purple Onion last night,' said Don, 'your customers also judge you on every interaction with your company. Our judgement on the Purple Onion was based on "product", meaning the meal itself. And on the "place", which is everything to do with the environment, but also the "people".'

Acknowledging that the weighting of each leg might vary from time to time and in different situations, Don encouraged his friends not to complicate it unnecessarily for now. 'I'm just keen to impress the concept on you for now, as the detail will be worked out when we workshop that with your team,' he said. They each gave examples of their own personal experiences to illustrate and further prove the point.

'Yes, but I'll say it again, they're all B2C businesses,' said James. 'How does it work for us in the B2B world?'

'While the checklist detail will differ in "product" and "people", the big difference in B2B is "place",' said Don. 'The "place" for a B2C business is its premises, such as a shop, hotel, pub or restaurant. But for a B2B business, "place" is your route to market. There is a whole range of things on a check-list that will help you there, such as your delivery schedules, or how orders are placed, or your telephone protocol. But that's an exercise for back home. I think it'd be good for you to convene a cross-functional project team to go through every touchpoint, and agree what best practice is.'

'That would be great for getting buy-in and engagement,' said Clare. 'We wouldn't possibly be able to do that without the teams. And let's not forget about our digital platform in all of that. We should include the website and our new online ordering platform too,' she added.

'Look, I hear you,' said James. 'But again, that sounds like a one-off project to me. How does that change the level of consistency so it happens all of the time?'

'This will take time,' said Don. 'After all, this organisation has been around for some time and you have habits that are embedded in your collective DNA. That's not to suggest that they are all bad habits, I should add. It's just that we have to shift mindsets and culture so that everyone in the organ-isation prioritises customers' needs over GTD's needs, or their own needs. By involving all departments, it gives everyone a voice in looking back in at themselves. It also gives each department an opportunity to call out obsta-cles that they see in each other's departments,' he added.

'You mean, put them into a bun-fight? That'll be fun,' said James.

'Well of course not' replied Don. 'I'll facilitate the first few meetings to establish a structured approach and to maintain decorum and respect. But I'll come back to that a little later if you don't mind. For now, I'm just keen to show how culture impacts your real world!'

LANESBOROUGH TO LOUGH REE

After coffee, James took the helm once again and they continued south on their journey into Lough Ree. 'Lough Ree, or the Lake of Kings,' said Don, 'is the third largest lake on the Shannon. It has about 50 islands, many of them with old ruins of castles and other Norman relics. It's about thirty-two kilometres long and six kilometres wide. That should be enough water for the Lough Ree monster,' he added, with a pause.

'Yes, right!' said James cynically. 'You Irish will do anything to attract a few tourists.'

'Well this story was told on BBC in 1960,' laughed Don. 'And they said it's probably the most credible of all such stories, even more than the Loch Ness monster. Anyway, the story goes that three priests were fishing on the lake in May 1960 and spotted a serpent-like creature, about six feet in length. So with the BBC and the Catholic priests being involved in the story, there can be no doubt,' he laughed.

'Enough water is right,' said James. 'I've just noticed on the echo sounder that the depth of the riverbed is more than 100 feet here.'

Don also told the story of the many battles in this area, some of them between the Dublin Vikings and their sworn enemies, the Vikings from Limerick, and other battles between the Normans and local Irish clans. 'So, conflict is a reality in this world. There will always be opposing views with different agendas, but thankfully,' he added, 'they don't all have to involve axes and shields.'

'In addition to the three-legged stool, there are a few more points I want to make,' said Don. 'While the stool gives us a framework and a checklist of things to consider under "product", "people" and "place", let me add some concepts that wrap around all of that.'

'When I refer to the three-legged stool as a framework, we also have to consider whether you want to be two, three, four or five star in your brand positioning. That will help to decide the answers to all the questions posed by the checklist. For example, if you want to be two or three star, then don't bother with an online ordering platform. But if you want to have a strong brand and be known for consistently great service, then you have to make appropriate decisions that reflect that positioning. The three-legged stool gives you a framework and a checklist to aid you in making those decisions.'

He paused and went on to add, 'I should tell you however that the trend around the world in all sectors, and regardless of whether you see yourself as two, three or whatever star rating, customer expectations are increasing. Consequently, every business needs to improve its offering. That's why I'm convinced more than ever before, that putting customer at the heart of all decision-making is now a basic ingredient for doing business. You simply have no choice. And remember too what we said earlier about "customer experience being the new battleground"?'

He left the thought hanging there and took out another piece of rice paper to perform his ceremony. He wrote,

'Premium is the New Black.'

Don went on to explain five additional points to watch out for in a B2B world and specifically in GTD.

'One:' he said, 'the services or products you sell need to be relevant to your target market. If the range of product is not sufficiently wide enough to warrant a buyer's time, or if the products don't match their needs, why should they bother with you?'

'Two: service providers should be transparent. That means they should be honest, own up to mistakes and follow through on promises.'

Seeing no resistance so far, Don continued. 'Three: the level of effort with which to do business with you should be low. In GTD's case, many of your customers work weekends and may want to be able to place an order 24/7. So if that means using technology, so be it. Not only that, all touchpoints should tell the same story. For example, the prices and availability information should be the same online, from the sales representative and from the contact centre.'

Clare said, 'Well, we have some work to do there.'

'Four:' said Don, 'customers expect consistency from their suppliers. Agreed delivery schedules should be like clockwork. The messages at every customer touchpoint, from the marketing messages through to delivery drivers, should be the same. Remember too that there are multiple contact points between a supplier and a customer from sales, to deliveries, to accounts.'

'Last but not least:' said Don, 'the personal touch means something too. After all, people buy from people, which should be acknowledged by developing personal relationships. Family businesses in particular have an opportunity to exploit this. James, it'd be good for you to go out and meet customers more and to accompany the sales guys and even the delivery drivers from time to time.'

'Yes, you're right,' admitted James. 'I don't get out to meet customers half enough.'

Knowing that a lot of new thinking had been shared, Don allowed some silence while they each took in the surroundings. As they passed Inchmore Island, he wrote on another piece of rice paper.

'B2B customers expect and value great experiences, just as much as in the world of B2C.'

Don added, 'There is another aspect of customer experience that I'd like you to consider. All of your customers are buying your products, so that they can sell them on, for a profit. What do you think GTD could be doing to help them with that?'

'I won't fall into the trap of saying best prices,' smiled James. 'But you know something? I have to admit I never really gave that any thought before, yet it's so obvious.'

'That's true,' added Clare. 'We're so insular in our thinking. All we focus on is selling our products in to our customers. We never really engage in any activity to help them sell out. That is an example of not putting our customer at the heart of our decision-making.'

James said 'In fairness, we do some marketing activity, which is probably more about building the brand. We have monthly promotions that the sales guys are always screaming for, but I get it. We could flip some of that activity to merchandising and point-of-sale material for our customers to promote our bakery products for example. Or perhaps we could offer some product training for their teams? I suppose that would show them that we care about them.'

'For sure, that's exactly it,' said Don. 'I think there are two benefits in that. It will differentiate you from your competitors and it'll send a message to your own team that you are shifting your focus.'

'What other initiatives do you have in mind to help embed this?' asked Clare. 'To really embed customer-centricity as a value or guiding principle there has to be more to it than that.'

'Yes, there is indeed,' said Don. 'As we said earlier, refreshing culture does take time. There are a few more issues that I want to flag. I want to talk about your internal meetings and complaints management first.'

James and Clare outlined their current meetings matrix in GTD, the purpose of each meeting, who attends which and the frequency. On the face of it, all of that seemed to make sense. However, Don knew from his "discovery" project that there were issues to do with the behaviours at those meetings. However, he held his counsel on that matter, with the intention of returning to it another time.

'To what extent do you think you really consider your customers in those meetings?' asked Don. 'Let's start with the end of each year when you do your budgets for the following year.'

'To be honest', said James, 'that exercise is where we build up our numbers, based on previous year's performance and new product ranges.'

'And do you take the time to consider changes in the external market-place, and how your customers and indeed their consumers are changing?' asked Don.

'No, we don't' said Clare flatly. 'It's a number crunching exercise more than anything. Isn't that true?' she asked James.

After an extended pause, James replied, 'I guess what you're saying is that we should really explore all you describe.'

Clare added 'And even that exercise alone would send a significant message to the senior team that we are moving away from insular thinking.'

'Precisely,' said Don. 'There are two wins in that. One is that people will realise that customers and their changing needs do matter and should be part of your big-picture thinking. Secondly, budgets are not plans. Budgets are a set of numbers that illustrate the score of the game you want to win. But from a cultural perspective, we want your senior team to role model a new culture and a different way of thinking.'

'There's something that I'm concerned about that comes to mind,' said Clare. 'While you're making perfect sense, is calling it out as a value or guiding principle really enough? Don't you think that some people will be cynical and not go along with it?'

'I know the answer to that one,' interjected James. 'I just won't accept it. We can show them the door!'

'But that is not the culture we want either, is it?' said Clare. 'Where people are being hired and fired all over the place.'

Don could feel the tension and to help smoothen it out, he said 'There is another way. Let's talk about measurement, first of all. In the same way that you measure sales and margin, by product categories and by territories, let's look at how you can measure if the company is being customer-centric.'

'Yes, what gets measured gets done,' said James.

'So are you suggesting that we do an annual survey?' asked Clare.

'I am' said Don. 'Not only does it send a message to your customers that you care about their views, but it also gives you gold dust in terms of insights.'

'And of course,' added Clare, 'we also have to be seen by our customers and by our own teams, to act on the feedback. Otherwise, we'll be the laughing stock of the trade.'

'If this survey is properly done, and the feedback is appropriately detailed, you can then include the scores in your leaders' individual objectives. For example, if you were to see a downward trend in the scores for deliveries, that gives you reason to have a challenging conversation with your operations manager. And even if he tries to blame another department, that at least puts the issue on the table so that you can get the right people in the room to fix it,' said Don.

'It shouldn't stop there either,' added Clare. 'That also needs to cascade throughout the organisation. We need to make sure that some element of service gets included in everybody's objectives.' After a pause, she added, 'but does this all sound very hard and aggressive?'

'Well if that was all you were doing,' replied Don, 'yes, I'd agree with you. But you can balance this with internal service level agreements between key departments. And you might also include incentives. It's about how you present it to your teams. And if it's okay with you, we'll go through that in detail when we meet the team.'

'Incentives?' shouted James. 'But that's more money. What about our margins?'

'Aw James, come on, we're not talking about the family jewels here,' said Don. 'Incentives are not always about money anyway. If we scratch our heads enough, I'm sure we will come up with cost-effective ideas. Besides,' he said after a short pause 'what about the cost of not doing it?'

Don deliberately left that big thought in the air for a few minutes. They were approaching the turn for Glasson, so he guided James through the exit from the main river. 'But of course,' said Don 'doing surveys or monitoring complaints is a complete waste of time, if you don't use the findings to do root cause analysis and take corrective actions. And by having a steering group that is constantly working on this, that will create enough positive noise too.'

Clare added another thought. 'All of the things you mentioned, Don, are hard to argue. And it's somewhat overwhelming, there is so much to do and there is so much change that we need to make. But it strikes me that all these changes are people related, is that how you see it?'

'Most of them are indeed, Clare. But there are some process changes too,' said Don. 'But let's agree again, that this trip is just about getting our heads around it all for now. The detailed planning and training will happen when we get into the action-planning workshop.'

'That's actually another point,' said Clare. 'Training. We don't take training seriously enough. Even when we hire new people, we throw them into the deep end from day one.'

'And what's wrong with that?' asked James. 'It worked for me. I don't believe in this training lark. Let them sink or swim. They can fight or take flight, I say!'

Looking towards Don, Clare raised her eyes to the heavens as Don winked back and smiled. 'All of this would be overwhelming if it was just the two of you involved. But don't forget we are transforming the culture, which involves everyone. The whole organisation,' said Don. 'We're just painting the picture for now.'

'So what do you think, guys? Based on all we have discussed this morning, can we agree that we need to have a value or guiding principle that calls out "customer"?' asked Don.

Without hesitation and with conviction, Clare answered 'Yes, for sure. Absolutely!'

James busied himself with navigating some turns, but didn't respond.

Mmm, he's not fully bought in to this yet, thought Don as he looked with pursed lips towards Clare. Clare just raised her eyebrows as if to say 'We're not there yet!'

As he checked the map for specific details for navigating to the Wineport Lodge for lunch, Don thought about what had been discussed so far. He was happy that everything that he planned to cover had indeed been covered. He was delighted with but not surprised by Clare's support. While James was still resisting somewhat, Don was not surprised that he hadn't yet made the jump. He knew that this would happen in increments, so long as all of the points could be proven to link back to sales and margin numbers. James is a very astute businessman and has an incredible feel for his own business. Getting him to embrace this feedback and to change was going to be an uphill climb.

However, knowing what was yet to come, Don continued to brace himself as he wrote another message on rice paper.

'Achieving long-lasting change of culture is not a project with a beginning and an end. It's an ongoing programme.'

5

RESPECT

Wineport Lodge: Lunchtime

James slowed the boat on approach to the mooring at Wineport. Hearing the short, high grunts of the ring-necked ducks, Clare walked along the side rail of the boat to the bow, to savour the rough beauty of the common reeds, the Sweet Flag and Yellow Irises.

Sitting snugly on the east side of Lough Ree in a very quiet location, surrounded by water and native woodland, sits the award-winning Wineport Lodge. It is a cosy hotel and restaurant famous for its casual luxury, with its own jetty to welcome the many boaters who frequent it. Clad all round with cedar, the building would remind you of the log cabins you'd see in the Swiss Alps. The Wineport name goes back to 542AD, when St Ciaran and his fellow monks are said to have used it as the perfect landing for their precious cargo of wine barrels from France.

Just up the road is the village of Glasson, which was built in the 1700s to service the local grand house known as Waterstown House. Now dilapidated, Don told his guests that it is now an attraction for ghost-busters who claim to have seen ghosts dancing on the site of the old ballroom.

On hearing more of Don's local folklore, James quipped 'Don, you're really milking it now. Lough Ree monsters, intelligent salmon and now the Waterstown ghosts, will you pull the other one?'

Clare and Don laughed heartily as Don tied the ropes and locked the boat. Don then decided to "pull the other one" by saying, 'Don't be surprised if you see a TV crew in the car-park. There was another sighting of the Lough Ree monster that went out on Sky News yesterday morning.'

With a look of total shock and disbelief, James did indeed see TV trucks, but Don chose not to tell him that the Wineport is the venue for a national TV programme called *The Restaurant*. He had been warned in advance when making the reservation that there would be some disruption.

Before entering the premises, the trio went for a short walk around the grounds. On passing the TV crew in the car park, they overheard a kerfuffle between an older technician and a younger one. The older one was displeased with his younger colleague for dropping a piece of kit. He shouted and roared at him, calling him all sorts of names beginning with "F", and with a few other choice words thrown in for good measure. The young lad, whose name was not Freddie or anything else beginning with "F", responded with equal passion. With a venomous voice, he too let loose a few "F" words, and stormed off.

With a look of disgust and disdain, James frowned and shook his head as he looked towards Clare and Don. 'What an ass!' said James, referring to the older technician. Clare then searched Don's deadpan expression for any acknowledgement or surprise.

James can be a difficult character. While highly passionate about the business and commercially savvy, he also has a reputation for being impatient, stubborn and for being a tough boss. Clare knows that deep down he is very caring and his bark is worse than his bite. Nevertheless, she has had to intervene and arbitrate on countless occasions when he has flown off the handle. And he is unbiased about who gets the brunt of his wrath and that, unfortunately, includes her and their kids occasionally.

Don also got a sense of this from his own experiences and interactions with James. More importantly however, he received numerous negative comments from the teams during the discovery phase about James' style. And to add fuel to that fire, there are a number of other managers who now exhibit a similar style. But of course that's no surprise, thought Don. 'Monkey see, monkey do.'

As it was only a few hours since having a hearty Irish breakfast, they all ordered a light lunch. Clare had the fried chicken and kale Caesar salad. James ordered the sourdough ciabatta and Don decided on the linguine pasta. Don eventually brought the conversation around to the recently completed Workbly employee survey. Knowing the answer in advance, he asked James and Clare, 'Tell me about your human resources key performance indicators? I'm curious to know what you think.'

'Gosh, to be honest Don, we don't have too many and the ones we do have, well we hardly ever look at them. Why do you ask?' said Clare.

'Well it's like this,' said Don. 'Your products account for about 62 percent of your total overheads, and you measure the performance of every item to within an inch of its life, right? Your delivery costs, which you outsource, account for about 6 percent and you monitor that very closely too. As it happens, your payroll investment accounts for approximately 20 percent of your overheads. I'm sure you'll agree therefore that it deserves monitoring too?' he added.

'I like that little deliberate slip of the tongue there Don,' smiled James. 'Investment indeed. Why not call it as it is, it's a cost!'

'Well, whatever way you see it,' said Don, 'Where my head is at, it deserves a lot more consideration than it's probably getting right now. In the same way that you expect a return from your other overheads, you should rightly expect a return on your payroll too,' he added.

'Aha,' said James. 'Now you're talking. I thought you were going off on one there, with some claptrap HR stuff. I know you're an independent consultant Don, but I don't want you acting like a freelance nuisance,' laughed James.

Don smiled and added, 'I don't believe there is a contradiction between maximising return on payroll and having a highly-engaged team.'

Don continued after a short pause, 'As with all elements of a survey like this, you have a lot of good stuff going on that you should be proud of. You have 55 percent of your people who are highly engaged; however there are 18 percent who are actively disengaged. That means that you have 27 percent who are neither engaged or disengaged. So they could swing either way, depending on which of the other groups impresses them most.'

'Explain that to me again,' said Clare.

'Okay, so what the survey is saying is that you have a large cohort of your people, 55 percent, who are totally with you on your "GTD bus." They are committed, proactive, big fans, proud and will adapt to appropriate change when needed. Now once again, that's great,' said Don.

'You have another smaller group, 18 percent, who feel somewhat negative towards the company. They are the ones who, for whatever reason, will moan and groan, they will resist change, complain regularly, either in public or in small groups.'

'Gosh,' said Clare, 'that group would be like a cancer in any organisation. Because negative people tend to be more vocal a lot of the time, they'd upset the apple-cart and affect morale. After all, good positive people are too busy getting the job done to be getting involved in gossip!' she added.

'Precisely,' said Don. 'That's it in a nutshell.'

'That is very disappointing,' added James. 'We pay everybody the market rate and many more above the rate. So what's the problem?' he asked. 'I suppose it's telling us straight to our faces that it's not all about money!' said Clare.

'I had a hotel client recently who told me that a kitchen porter moved to another employer for 20c per hour,' said Don. 'Now think about that: over a forty-hour week, that person will earn an extra €8 per week, before tax. Plus, they now have an extra thirty minutes commute each way. So would you say they really left for 20c per hour?'

'Of course not,' said Clare. 'The 20c masked the real issue, whatever that was.'

'Now think too,' added Don, 'about the impact the disengaged might have on your customers, on company progress, on new ideas. While working with a retailer recently, I met with a disgruntled sales associate who is so annoyed with his employer that he does not report theft he sees by customers or by colleagues.'

'But that's sabotage!' said James.

'Yes, it is James, and I'm not at all condoning it. But it's real life. And let me add that customers are expert at spotting when somebody is not happy in their job. Now I'm not scaremongering here, it's all fixable. But can we agree that it needs attention?'

'Then what is the bloody problem with them?' asked James. 'Why are they disengaged?'

'Let me give you some more feedback,' said Don. 'There are some operational and communication issues that are partly causing it. But many of those can be addressed back at base. That includes equipment and resources, the quality of planning and some things like that. Honestly, the scores for those elements were not bad, but they do need attention. However it's the categories on leadership, communications and culture that concern me.'

'There's one thing that I feel needs attention,' said Clare 'and that's the silos we have. I just wish that people and their departments collaborated some more and recognised that we're all here for the same reason. Instead, they get entrenched and defensive within their own departments and blame the others. We had a late delivery issue with our biggest customer recently. It escalated to their operations director, as it wasn't the first time we let them down. And I know that it caused all sorts of ructions in our place. The sales guys delighted in blaming the warehouse. The warehouse immediately blamed the contact centre and the IT system. It's all so stressful and unnecessary.'

'What was that all about?' asked James. 'I was never told about that.'

'Look, it's all sorted now,' said Clare. 'We'll talk about the detail another time. But it's just another example of a deep-rooted problem and it's definitely now a morale issue,' she added.

'I think you're right,' said Don. 'This is a very sensitive area that needs to be carefully managed. Things like this can have a huge impact on the emotional commitment of your people to the company, hence the worrying HR key performance indicators. Your absenteeism is at about 5–6 percent, which is above the industrial average, and last year your non-managers employee turnover was 28 percent. All of that has a cost that affects your bottom line.'

Clare added, 'Now that is very true. James, you yourself just recently complained about our recruitment costs last year.' Then Don added, 'and it also affects your employer brand reputation, after all people do talk and post reviews online.'

Don was aware that he was landing some very strong messages. While very sensitive with his delivery, he was careful to bring balance and hope for recovery. But he also knew where it was all coming from. And he sensed that Clare knew it too.

'To what extent do leaders and managers influence this?' asked Clare.

'Well that's it exactly Clare,' said Don. 'The management style and the behaviours that frontline managers role model are highly significant. I have seen it time and time again. The best managers get great employee survey scores, they also tend to get great customer service scores and they deliver on their numbers, almost every time! The co-relation is really strong. Their people really *want* to deliver for their bosses. And that's engagement,' he added.

'But Don, is this engagement lark all getting hyped up with these tech companies offering employment terms that no traditional business could ever match? Bloody beanbags, free beer and flexible working. They're the ones that are filling the heads of these millennials and Gen Zers with expectations that are just unrealistic and not for the real world,' fumed James.

'They're not all as cosy as you think James. One of the big name tech companies that has a reputation for all you described had a strike and walk-out in the last couple of years,' said Don. 'And not only that, I know of some traditional companies that went out and bought fuzz-ball machines for their people in the hope of improving engagement. But apart from a short positive spike, nothing changed in practice. Productivity remained low, and people turnover remained high. You see, those incentives have short-term impact if people are being treated badly by their bosses or their peers.'

'I wonder has the new trend of working from home post-lockdown changed that in any way?' asked Clare.

'Well, it's funny you should mention that,' said Don. 'I listened to a discussion about that on our national radio station recently. The interviewer was chatting with an anonymous panel of employees of tech companies from around the world. As a result of working from home, they now realise that the free beer and other perks are masking the real culture. And that culture has fear, blame and silos at its core.'

'There you go,' said James. 'I knew it couldn't be a bed of roses. That scene just didn't add up for me.'

As the coffee arrived, Don said, 'there is a key word here that I believe is the common denominator for all we've discussed. And you may need to consider a value or guiding principle linked to this. That word is "respect".'

'I completely agree,' said James, far too quickly, 'some of these people have no respect. No respect at all.'

Clare added very tentatively, to nobody in particular, 'Yes, but to gain respect, you have to show respect.'

As silence descended, Don knew, that James knew, that the comment was directed at him. And he allowed it to linger while he called for the bill.

As they reboarded the boat and settled back in, Don took out the rice paper.

'To gain respect, you have to show respect.'

GLASSON TO ATHLONE

Don started the engines and pulled away very gently. The weather was still good and he was so pleased that the boat offered temporary distractions. James wound up the rope at the bow and Clare did the same at the stern. Don said, 'We're going back in to Lough Ree and taking a left turn south through Athlone.'

Don went on to describe Athlone, which is steeped in history due to its location in the centre of the country. It was a physical divide between the old clans of Connacht, west of the Shannon, and those from Leinster and Munster. Today, it's a busy town with quite a number of pharmaceutical giants, due to the availability of a highly educated workforce within a one-hour drive. 'This town has certainly come a long way since the Viking Olaf Scabbyhead plundered it in 933,' said Don. That prompted a laugh and more chat about the Vikings and brought a little light relief to a somewhat tense atmosphere. Don continued to navigate through the channel into the lake, down past the anglers hidden in the rushes on the west side, under the M6 bridge and onwards towards the town.

As he invited James to once again take the wheel, Don brought the conversation back to Disney from the day before. 'Remember I mentioned Disney's value chain, and that customer satisfaction is their relentless goal? Well guess what they believe is the main driver of that customer satisfaction?' Before either of his guests fell into the obvious trap and gave the wrong answer, he said, 'It's employee satisfaction, or, as they call it, "cast satisfaction". They measure it every year, just like you did recently with your Workbly survey.'

'So they mollycoddle them! You can't say boo to these young ones anymore,' said James, now back to his usual form. 'I wouldn't say that,' said Don. 'They pay their people the going rate in the theme park industry and other terms are also on par with the market. They expect high productivity from their people but they also know that high levels of engagement deliver that for them,' he added.

'Knowing where we are at right now, Don, what do you think we have to do in GTD to get our people more engaged?' asked Clare.

'Well,' said Don. 'Let's agree that employee engagement, trust and respect go hand in hand. And can we also agree that respect can be interpreted very differently by different people? But for now, let's focus on basic things like how people are spoken to. By that I mean tone of voice. And it also includes such things as how we communicate with them, that is, if they feel included and consulted appropriately, and so on. That all affects the way they are made to feel.'

Just then, Don noticed a small rowing boat approximately 70 metres ahead directly in front of them, with a lone angler facing away from them. Knowing that James too had seen him, he winked at Clare and then roared at James. 'James! What in the name of God are you doing? Will you watch where you're going. You have to be vigilant at all times. You can't be looking around you as if you own the bloody river,' he snarled.

With total and utter shock, James got into a flap and mistakenly pushed the throttle forward instead of back. Don reached over to rescue the situation, although their speed was no threat. James shouted back at Don, 'What the hell did I do wrong? I saw the damn boat and I had it totally under control.'

Don moved away for fear of meeting James' fist with his face. He then smiled at James and said nothing. He allowed a prolonged silence for James to regain his composure and to let the message sink in.

Clare thought it best to say nothing and let this play out.

'James,' said Don. 'I knew you were in total control. I saw you getting ready to steer around the angler. I set you up. I'm really sorry, but I did it for a reason. Now tell me honestly, how did you feel when I spoke down to you like that?'

With a little sulk and an air of acceptance, James said, 'Okay, I get it. So I'm the problem then.'

Now if James was hoping for someone to tell him he was wrong, he was sadly mistaken. Both Clare and Don knew that if James could shift his thinking and then his behaviours, things would get a lot better for the business. And for the family, thought Clare.

'James, you are quite brilliant as a CEO. Look where you and Clare have taken the business since taking it over from your father. And look at how successful the bakery has become, something your father disagreed with. You are one of the leading players in your industry and you've been very profitable for years. So let's get a balance here. The passion that you bring is relentless and infectious. And it's that and your understandable impatience that drives it forward. So let's be very clear about that,' said Don.

'But why is my tone a problem now all of a sudden?' asked James.

'Well, perhaps it's not just now,' said Don. 'Everyone reacts differently to that style. Some of your managers now mimic your best characteristics and they also drive the business. However, some of them have also recognised that the way to get on is to be brusque and tough. So they are actually being rewarded for being rude! But times are changing and that style of management just doesn't cut it anymore. I don't need to tell you that. And before you say it,' he laughed, 'I don't mean mollycoddling them.'

'For example, let's look back at the incident we saw with the TV crew in the Wineport. How do you think that young lad felt being castigated in public like that?' asked Don. James just nodded while Don continued, 'And you saw how he reacted. He just told his boss to "f-off" and walked away.'

'But it's the way I am! People know that I just want the best for the business, and for their jobs,' said James.

'Yes, I know you mean well,' said Clare. 'But you don't always have to keep it a secret!'

James scowled at her.

Don interrupted, 'James, the negative impact of that style on your business is just too great. That atmosphere causes a blame culture, people get defensive, it creates silos and it stifles real progress. People will conform for their own protection and not raise their head above the parapet. It puts all the pressure on you to come up with the big ideas. And it means you have to micro-manage. That's not going to help your ambition to stand back and plan your exit.'

Don knew that this was very painful for James. But he had a duty of care to be frank and honest with him. He delivered his message with a soft tone and genuine compassion. James, Clare and Don were of a similar vintage. Don's own journey had not been a bed of roses so he had lots of empathy for James and his predicament.

James seemed deflated, and after a prolonged pause he said, 'I hear you. And I'm genuinely taking this all in. I'd hate to think that people feel that I don't respect or regard them, because it's just not true. But I just don't know if this leopard can change its spots.'

'Of course you can James. Feedback is the breakfast of champions,' said Don, as he tapped James warmly on his back. 'You are surrounded by people who care about you and the business. I know this is the first time you've done a project like this and perhaps you weren't expecting this, and nor was I by the way. But we work with what we have. Let me say again, this is all fixable. I promise! And I should add, this is not the only challenge, so don't feel it's all about you,' he added.

As they approached Athlone Lock, Don suggested that they moor the boat and go for a little glass of Guinness in Sean's Bar, the oldest pub in Ireland. Before leaving, Don wrote on a piece of rice paper.

'There is no contradiction between seeking maximum productivity and high levels of engagement.'

SEAN'S BAR, ATHLONE

After settling into the tiny pub, Clare said, 'So back to my question. What do we have to do to improve engagement?'

'First of all,' said Don. 'I want you to consider another value or guiding principle around "respect". For all the reasons we've already discussed, it will make a significant difference to your culture and you'll win all the way. In fact, let's call it a win-win. You'll win personally, the business will win and your team of almost 200 people will win.'

If only, thought Clare. Throughout all of this discussion, she knew the elephant in the room had to come up.

'Well, I'm all for it, so long as we can truly bring it to life in our day-to-day,' she said.

46

Without hesitation and with no holding back, James said, 'I agree. And I really do mean that.'

'There are so many ways that you can show that you're a respectful and caring organisation and that you do genuinely value your people. But when refreshing your culture, we need a framework. Let me introduce you to what I call the HR mix,' said Don.

'Clare, you asked how we bring it to life and we'll do that by focusing on the elements that influence engagement and productivity. Now of course leadership is important, but let's start with the first pillar of the HR mix. Let's talk about how we can show respect by having the right person in the right job. By that I'm referring to your organisational structure.'

'We have that covered off, haven't we Clare?' said James.

'Yes, you do have very detailed structure charts,' said Don. 'But they don't always match reality or what the business really needs. You have some people in boxes who got the role because of their longevity in the business. But are they the right fit in that role for where the business is going? If you were to start from scratch, would you really give them all the jobs they are currently in? You have also hired new people recently without even apparently considering internal applicants,' said Don. 'There is a better way to do that so that people feel respected and have opportunities to grow and develop in the business. They need to know that they can have a future in this business.'

'Aha, so you want us to fire some people? Now who's the tough guy?' quipped James.

'Of course not,' said Don. 'But every organisation should take time out now and then to revisit their organisational structure. After all, you have a set of budgets and forecasts for the business. You have new product streams in addition to the bakery. You have an online presence that you didn't have before.'

'Yes,' said Clare. 'We didn't really change the structure when that was launched.'

Don continued, 'And if you reassess your structure, you may not change anything about the boxes on the organisational charts, but you just might change some of the people. The last thing you should do is fire anybody and lose all the goodwill they bring. Perhaps some of those who are in the wrong boxes could even be redeployed in other roles that are more suited to their skill sets.'

'Yes I know what you're referring to,' said Clare. 'James, we went outside to hire a regional manager for the northern region and we knew that some of the sales guys wanted that job. It did cause a lot of back-biting and resentment. I feel badly for that new manager.'

'We didn't have the time for that,' snapped James. 'But before you say it, I hear you. We should have planned that well in advance. Anyway, to promote one of those sales guys would have been a disaster. They would have been useless. Great salespeople don't always make great managers. There is a whole different set of skills required in being a manager to being a great salesperson,' said James.

'That's true and perhaps you're right. Maybe they wouldn't have been right this time,' said Don. 'But look at the optics of that! Perhaps if you had *shown some respect to them*,' he stressed, 'the organisation could have been clear about expectations for the role and actually helped the ambitious guys to apply in a fair and transparent process.'

'Yes,' said Clare, 'and an organisation that really cares about its people would have an ongoing succession plan. That would certainly show that we respect our own people and that we want them to get on. James, you were saying to me recently how bothered you were about our Sarah being in a dead-end job. Well it's not a dead-end company. They're going places, but they just haven't helped her develop a career path.'

Sarah is the apple of James' eye and Clare knew that would strike a chord with him.

'The next pillar of the HR mix is learning and development,' said Don. 'You have a great opportunity to show respect to your people by giving them the knowledge and skills to do the job. And James, I know you shared your views earlier on training. But I'm sure you didn't mean that,' he smiled.

Before he got the chance to argue, Clare quipped, 'of course he didn't. That's why he went for golfing lessons before that major tournament with his old college mates. He wasn't happy with his putting. And by the way, he won it.'

With that slam dunk, home run and hole in one for Clare, James just smiled. He was stumped and snared and he knew it.

'Look guys, as the American baseball pitcher Vernon Law said, "*Experience is a hard teacher because she gives the test first, the lesson afterwards.*" And it doesn't have to be like that anymore. Not only is it hard for your people, but think of the risk to your business! We all get training in all walks of life, it's just not always structured. I honestly believe that if you had an active training plan in your business, it would send an incredible message to your people. That shows respect in volumes,' he added.

'Before we go further, Clare, can you make a note to put a budget against that?' said James.

'That's great, James, but can we leave the detailed planning for another time? But can I add, it doesn't always have to be about money? There are other ways to skin the cat.'

'Go on,' said James.

'Well,' said Don, 'you might develop a coaching sub-culture, where you get your own seasoned senior people to mentor some of the more junior or newer ones. Now, they will have to get training for that and that will cost a few bob. But the cascading benefit from that investment would be enormous.'

'And that too would be very *motivational and respectful* for the mentors,' Clare stressed. They would feel great that their expertise and contribution is being recognised and valued.'

'Let's go, as I want to take you for a short walk around Athlone Castle before we go back to the boat. Just so you know,' he laughed as James gave him a funny look, 'it was originally a wood structure but the stone structure you see today was built in Norman times for King John in 1210. It is beautifully restored as an icon of ancient Ireland.'

After a short stop to take it in, Don continued, 'I also want to move on to the next HR pillar, which is "communications".'

As they walked, Don continued, 'James, I know you already mentioned that you have a structured meetings matrix. And I should tell you, that came up as a positive during my discovery. Most people rely on them for knowing what's going on and what the priorities are. Now that's obviously great.'

'Yes,' said James proudly. 'I run the weekly operations meeting myself and the monthly management meeting too, obviously. I think they work quite well. Don't you Clare?'

'Yes they do, James, I agree. But I know there's a "but" coming,' she smiled.

'Can I tell you,' said Don. 'Communications is the one topic that probably every organisation gets poor scores on. It's so difficult to get it right. Some people take umbrage when they don't know *exactly* what's going on.'

'Yes but come on now Don, you're not saying that we should be having meetings about meetings, are you?' asked James. 'No, not at all,' said Don. 'I am saying though that you can never over-communicate, especially in times of change. And of course, notwithstanding Covid and all that brought to the world, change is ongoing.'

Don continued, 'I know this is a really difficult one for every company. Some people get upset if they hear a piece of news from someone other than who they deem to be the appropriate person. Others do get included and then they forget they were told. And then you'll come across other situations where people feel they were not told on time. It's a hard one to win.'

'That's for sure,' said Clare. 'I know that I brief my team after every meeting and yet I overheard a conversation recently where one of my team denied being told about a big customer's request for changes to payment terms. Anyway Don, I know you're going to say that we shouldn't ignore it.'

'Well, that's it,' said Don. 'But there are easy tools to help you such as your fellow Englishman Rudyard Kipling's rhyme. *"I keep six honest serving-men. They taught me all I knew. Their names are What and Why and When and How and Where and Who".'*

James stopped walking. He looked at Don. He looked at Clare. He looked again at Don and then again at Clare as he threw his eyes to the heavens with a burst of laughter and said, 'Don. I've been listening to your bullshit since landing in Ireland. If it's not history lessons of old Ireland, which of course are very interesting, it's yarns about the Lough Ree monster. And now we have to listen to an Irishman quoting English literature. What are you like?'

Now with all three in hysterics, Don added, 'And we haven't even started on the rugby!'

As Don explained some more about using Kipling's 5Ws framework he went on to add, 'There is another topic in communications that I want to remind you of, and that's your annual performance reviews. I'm delighted that they are happening, so well done on that. So many companies struggle with these and it's hard to get them right. That said, it shows great respect when you take the time to give feedback, and listen openly to concerns and ambitions. I do think yours could be modernised and it won't take much to improve them some more.'

James said, 'I wonder is there too much emphasis put on communications, Don? People should know well what they have to do and what's going on.'

'Possibly,' said Don. 'But when you don't manage the formal communications from the centre with newsletters, meetings, notice-boards, intranet or whatever, the bush-telegraph takes over. And then the rumour-mill can become the pseudo-official channel.'

'That's very true,' said Clare. 'We should take a leaf from our customers' book. In most hotels, they have a daily briefing when the head of function briefs her or his team on the priorities for the day ahead.'

'Exactly right,' said Don. 'In fact, we should look at communications as an opportunity to inform and inspire, not just something that we "have" to do.'

Don continued, 'We should also try to be even more transparent. That means explaining the rationale behind internal changes and decisions. People don't just want to do what is expected of them but they also want to know why they're doing those things and where they fit into the big picture. Make it safe for them to propose constructive ideas and then listen to them. That's respect.'

Clare chimed in 'All of that makes sense to me, James. To be honest, none of this is rocket science. It's basic common sense really.'

'It is Clare,' said Don. 'But I'm afraid common sense is not always common practice.'

'Ouch,' said James.

'What I mean by that,' said Don quickly, 'is that when leaders are busy doing the day job they can often overlook the basic skills of leadership. It's not that they intend to be forgetful of people's feelings. But the effect of them not remembering can appear like they're taking their people for granted.'

'That's true,' said Clare. 'And that's not good.'

'The fourth and last—but not least—pillar, is "wellbeing",' said Don. 'This includes reward, recognition, general wellbeing, and of course diversity and inclusion.'

'Gosh, that's a mouthful,' said Clare.

'It is, but I can tell you, you are well up there on diversity. And when you think of the various global "diversity and inclusion" movements in recent years, just keep doing what you're doing,' said Don.

'Let's focus on the other bits that link to respect,' he continued. 'Starting with reward, I have no feedback for you in that regard. The only ongoing watch-out is that you are fair and consistent. If team members were to find out that their peers doing similar jobs were paid more, then they would immediately feel disrespected.' James and Clare nodded in agreement.

'Do you know I had a case recently with another client, a hotel, that had completed a Workbly employee survey. Two things stood out for me. The canteen facilities were slated and the complaints about financial reward were plenty. Then six months later, we did a resurvey to find that both scores had increased. When I met the client to give the feedback, I asked if they had worked on both of those issues in the meantime. It turns out that they had significantly improved the canteen facilities, changing the menu and freshening up the place. So I asked again if they had given their people an increase. And they hadn't.'

He left that thought in the air before continuing, 'Now, think about that! When employees are dissatisfied with work conditions, they often complain about money. It's as if to say "I don't get paid enough to work with this crap." But when you listen to them and pay due respect by improving conditions or eliminating obstacles, they feel more engaged. Then money is less of an issue.'

'Wow,' said James. 'I get it and to think it was staring us in the face all this time. Gosh, how did I miss that?' he added.

'Recognition on the other hand, is quite an emotional issue. And this is in the gift of the frontline managers. They are the ones who should know when a person goes above and beyond the call of duty. That might be as simple as staying back late to process an order or putting their hands up to own a project. Now this is an area where there is room for improvement. Do you know that you have one manager who never even says hello to the team members in the morning? And not only that, the manager is seen to be rude and often disparaging with comments to the team. And what the manager says about peers in management behind their backs is quite shocking. Apparently only ever focusing on the negatives. This manager was actually named in the Workbly survey, but I blacked out the name.'

'I can guess who that is,' snapped James.

'Well, I'm not going to get into that,' said Don. 'But as we said before, that culture permeates. And James, I have to be honest, if you know who it is, then you need to ask yourself why this wasn't dealt with before?'

Feeling scolded, James said, 'Look Don, this whole process is an epiphany for me. Honestly and truly. I was sceptical at first about it. And while I'm not saying I agree with everything you're saying, I really can see the importance of having the right culture. One that is proactively designed by us and lived every day. It's going to be hard work to change it, but I agree it has to happen.'

Energised by James' apparent transformation, Clare interjected, 'James, you're right. It will be hard work. But it's absolutely the right thing to do. If we crack it, it's actually going to make life a lot easier with less tension and firefighting. I'm so looking forward to having a framework within which people will be expected to behave. And I know it's not going to turn them into robots but it'll be like a checklist for us all to abide by.'

She paused and then continued, 'And I'll bet you it'll impact our bottom line too.'

Clare had one more point to make as she brought the discussion around to flexible hours and home-working. 'The lockdown due to Covid-19 taught us many things,' she said. 'But when I see how productive we were with people working from home and their comfort with online communications platforms, it's something that we should continue with.'

James seemed like he was about to disagree, so Clare cleverly jumped back in again to say, 'I think it shows great respect to those with kids or long commutes. Even our own Sarah said she found it a welcome change.' The mention of his darling daughter put a stop to any negative comment that James might have made.

They arrived back to the boat and while James excused himself to make a call, Don wrote on some rice paper.

'Respect should be remembered in all elements of the HR mix; that includes right person – right job, training, communications and wellbeing.'

Clare said to Don, 'I think we're making real progress here. This is great but there is an elephant that we cannot ignore.'

'Yes, I know,' said Don. 'You're referring to your kids, right? Can I suggest not to bring it up for now? I think that James will bring it up himself when the time is right. If he doesn't, I promise you, I'll find a way.'

'Sorry about that,' said James on his return. 'I had to call the very manager I think we were talking about.' With a startled look from Clare, he added, 'Don't worry, I didn't say a word. It was about something else.'

'That actually brings me close to finishing on issues that impact respect. Let's not forget about leadership,' said Don. 'In times of crisis such as with Covid-19, the imperative is to get cash and perhaps even to restructure. I believe that leaders can still do those things provided they are honest and transparent. In saying that, I find that leaders, generally speaking, regularly underestimate the impact of their own behaviours on other people. Middle management in particular are effectively operating in a fishbowl for all to see and make judgements on. And that's genuinely tough for them. They often get caught between senior leaders and their own teams. But they need to be role models for the right behaviours, yet they often overlook that. Too often they send mixed messages and are far too inconsistent.'

He continued. 'That said, the good ones show real empathy and interest in their teams. They may not always remember the names of their cats, sick aunts, and their favourite holiday destinations. But they should show an interest in their wellbeing and progress. And talk to them. I saw a very credible study recently that showed that for 75 percent of participants, the most stressful part of their job was their direct manager. And that has a direct impact on productivity.'

'We clearly have work to do with our teams,' said Clare. 'If we are to make this culture refresh a success, they have a key role to play. So getting them on board and committed is essential.'

'Yes, it is indeed,' said Don. 'And we'll return to that, as that is all part of the "delivery" phase where we bring this all to life.'

As Don started up the engines and his guests did the ropes, he said in closing, 'So we're agreed then that "respect" needs to be called out as a value?'

'Absolutely, for sure,' responded James very quickly and convincingly. 'I suppose my concerns move now to how we bring this all to life and maintain momentum. I wouldn't be happy to put all this effort in just because of how the world has changed after Covid-19.'

'And of course you're right, James. I fully agree with you,' said Don. 'But first of all, even if the pandemic never happened, you should be doing this anyway. This is just best practice.'

'That's true,' said Clare. 'We were talking about some of this James even before the outbreak. But I guess the crisis highlighted the need even more.'

'Indeed,' said Don. 'In fact your culture gets tested every day, and even more so in a crisis.'

'But back to James' really good point. You said the word "momentum" and that's one essential ingredient in helping to embed this. The other is that we will have to explore how to make individuals, at all levels, accountable for their actions and their behaviours. And we'll explore that next,' he added.

ATHLONE LOCK

Don brought the boat slowly into the lock and waited for the water levels to drop and the gates to open. He repeated the benefits of putting people first and improving engagement. He reminded his guests of the potential improvement in morale, productivity, customer experience and reputation as a great employer.

As James and Clare nodded their agreement and again went to work with the ropes, Don sent a text from his phone. He reflected on the day so far and performed his ritual with more rice paper.

Respect

'Leaders who show respect build more trust – and engagement follows, leading to high productivity.'

He was happy that real progress was being made in agreeing the essential values that will make this business play like an orchestra. While it was a bit testy at times with James, who can be quite defensive, he was satisfied that the main feedback had landed safely. At least on the face of it, so far. He was also encouraged though by Clare's enthusiasm, after all, she knows him best.

But he knew what was ahead with regard to the family troubles. He had met Sarah and Tom during the discovery and he knows that Tom is very upset with his father. That would require very careful choreography to ensure that current tensions and bad feeling could be massaged. He was also concerned that if any new expectations were set, that they could be delivered on.

If that situation could be resolved, that'd be the icing on the cake, he thought.

6

ACCOUNTABILITY

ATHLONE TO CLONMACNOISE

As Don started the engines once again after the lock opened, he informed his upbeat guests that they were now heading to Clonmacnoise. Unsure whether it was the breakthrough that had just happened or the Guinness, he let his thoughts wane with the gentle breeze. The noise of the nearby weir and the town with its hustle and bustle was fading into the distance as they rounded the long bend in the river.

'We're running a little behind what I expected,' said Don. 'We're staying in Banagher tonight and we've a bit to go. But we have a little breeze behind us and the current gets a little faster in this stretch, so we should be okay. I'd really like us to make a short stop at Clonmacnoise. When you see it from the river, you yourselves will be disappointed if we don't stop.'

'Why is that?' asked James. 'Are we talking more Vikings or are we going to hear about leprechauns this time? You haven't mentioned anything about them yet!'

Don laughed heartily. In the months that James and Don had come to know one another, they had developed a really good rapport. They both had huge respect for each other and had a lot in common. The banter and friendly rivalry between Brits and Irish regularly came to the fore. Because of that, Don intended to make the most of this time together and tease James with Irish stories. After all, they were on his turf!

On a more serious note, Don knew that his feedback was sensitive and challenging. Despite the positivity he knew there was more challenge to come. So there was no time for complacency. He was glad to have some light-hearted distractions for balance.

'Well, funny you should mention that,' laughed Don.

Before he got to make his point, James interrupted 'Oh for God's sake,' as he then loudly sang a couple of lines of Queen's "We Are the Champions".

'Do you know something?' said James. 'You're going to laugh when I tell you this. I actually have some Irish blood in me.'

'Yes, you and millions of other hopefuls,' laughed Don.

'I'm serious,' said James. 'The name Drinkwater was actually a nickname that goes back to medieval times and it stuck. My ancestors are from Lancashire but my grandmother on my mother's side is from...' and he sang 'It's a Long Way to Tipperary.'

'Well that's not far from here, James, so you probably already know then that Clonmacnoise goes back to the time of St Ciarán in the sixth century, just after St Patrick introduced Christianity to Ireland,' said Don through the laughter. 'It is one of the oldest of the early Christian settlements in Europe. It was built in the centre of Ireland where at one time an ancient roadway crossed a shallower part of the River Shannon. For that reason, it had great strategic importance as a town and religious settlement. As you can imagine, the Vikings plundered it and then, sadly it was burnt down in the sixteenth century by the Anglo-Normans. Wait till you see the round tower. It's really impressive. We'll pop in for a look.'

'So you're blaming the Brits for this too?' exclaimed James.

'Aw James, it was another time and thankfully lots of water has gone under the bridge since then.'

'Or over it, in this case,' laughed James.

'It's funny you should mention the word "blame" however,' said Don. 'We're going to chat about that now if you don't mind?'

'Oh dear, but Don, just before you do,' interrupted Clare. 'I'm just thinking out loud here, we now have two values that we have more or less agreed to. What else do we have to do?' Because Clare knows James inside out and that he's an impatient man of action, she was keen to ask the question that she suspected might be percolating in his mind.

'There are another two topics that we need to discuss,' said Don. 'The heavy lifting, however, is in embracing the concept of culture in the first place. I'm sure the first two values that we covered already, "customer-centricity" and "respect", have helped you to see how they will shape the behaviours of your people. I'm confident that you'll find these next ones just as easy to digest. But remember, for now this trip is about taking the time to understand the positioning of culture in your overall business model.'

'I'm okay with that,' said Clare. 'I feel we've both got a good handle on what culture is by now.'

Don continued, 'Great, and it's also about building a set of draft values that you're comfortable with. And don't forget, we already got input from your teams. Nevertheless, we will engage your senior team in fine-tuning what we come up with and in the wordsmithing of the final set of values,' he added. 'So are you both still okay with that?'

Clare deliberately stayed silent this time and waited for James to reply, which he did warmly and positively. She was feeling very good as a result of the progress being made so far. But of course her mind immediately flipped to the issue with the kids and she tensed again. She was pleased that James had earlier acknowledged the issue and was delighted that he did that in front of Don. That gave her an ally that she didn't have before. She had already spoken privately to Don at length about this during the "discovery". She also knew that he had met with the kids separately and that they too were honest and open with him. She had come to realise that she was now very dependent on him, more than she had previously expected.

'I'd like to return to the "blame" issue and tell you about how I conducted the one-to-one meetings that I had with your teams,' said Don. 'In each case, I started by putting them at ease with social chat and their own career. That was all designed to build rapport and trust. I would then bring the interviewee on a journey of discussion on various aspects of their own job. I asked each of them to describe their role, and that in itself was enlightening.'

'What do you mean by that?' asked James.

'Well, quite often the person's title did not at all match the day-to-day job they were actually doing. Now that's very understandable for people who are with you for many years, as the business and their role evolves over time. For example, one of your key account sales team also has social media marketing in his remit, because he is young and happens to be interested in it. But then I asked him how he is measured at the end of the year, and he told me that it was sales only.'

'Yes,' said James. 'But what's wrong with that? After all, that's his main job, isn't it?'

'Yes it is of course,' said Don. 'Leave aside for now that he should also be measured on other key performance indicators, but we'll come back to that.

But let me ask you, who should be responsible for the success or otherwise of social media activities then?'

'Well it's the Head of Marketing, of course,' said James.

'That's probably correct,' said Clare. 'But James, remember the difficult review you had with Sue and how she tried to blame Rob for the unprofessional and inconsistent Twitter and Facebook posts?' James just nodded.

'I don't mean to use the Rob and Sue example as the "whipping boy" for this issue because it was quite prevalent in other parts of the business too,' said Don. 'I could also quote you other scenarios in other parts of the business. But they are just more examples of the same thing. The Workbly employee survey also pointed to the issue. And the issue I'm referring to is "accountability",' he added. 'As we have discussed with every issue so far, let me assure you, however, that this too is eminently fixable.'

James was starting to feel concerned. After a stellar few years of taking his father's business to the next level and making nice profits along the way, he now finds himself being told about all the things that are wrong with the business. This can't be right he thought, otherwise the business would have gone bust years ago. He knows that the issues to do with his tone of voice and the kids need attention. He hates that he has had tension with them and genuinely wants to improve it. But Tom in particular has such a different way of doing things. 'Dad, the world has changed,' he regularly says and that infuriates James. It makes him feel he's over the hill and not in tune with the modern world. And now, Don is also prodding and prodding.

'Don, you're giving us a lot of stuff to address here,' said James. 'I have to tell you, I'm beginning to wonder are these issues just a reality for any company and you're being pedantic in pointing them out?'

As Clare seemed to tense up, Don said softly, 'I can understand why you'd say that. And it's true. They are indeed evident in varying proportions in almost every business. But as customers' expectations continue to rise and your competitors are taking some of your market share, you have already agreed that you have to up your game. And remember, I'm not inventing these issues. Your customers and your own people have told you what they're not happy with.'

Clare interjected, 'James we shouldn't shoot down the message or the messenger. Remember why we're here. Profits have slipped and we need to get back on track before we move on with our lives in a few years. I'm much less concerned about whether other organisations have these issues or not. We have them in our business so that's enough for me. We have to address them.'

'That's it,' added Don. 'And I have to compliment you on how you're taking this feedback so far. I do appreciate that this can't be easy and I know I'm downloading a lot of information here, but you don't have to be overly concerned at this time. I promise, this will all come together very soon. But let's continue to use this private time together to understand the issues and the implications. As I said, we'll have lots of time to go through them in more detail back in HQ with your team. After all, you're going to need their support and commitment too.'

James relaxed and nodded his assent. Clare looked relieved as Don reminded himself to remain on his guard to James' reactions and feelings. He also decided to add some light relief and told this short story.

> There were four people named Everybody, Somebody, Anybody, and Nobody.
>
> There was a special job to be done and Everybody was sure that Somebody would do it.
>
> Anybody could have done it, but Nobody did it.
>
> Somebody got angry about that because it was Everybody's job.
>
> Everybody thought that Anybody could do it, but Nobody realised that Everybody wouldn't do it.
>
> It ended up that Everybody blamed Somebody when Nobody did what Anybody could have done.

Clare looked to James, then back to Don and said, 'Don, I'll challenge you to tell us that again after a glass of wine!'

'Not a chance,' said James. 'He'll be too busy concocting tomorrow's history lessons!'

Enjoying the banter, Don continued, 'If we can get every single person totally focused on the things that will drive the business forward and they are made fully accountable for their key performance indicators, the business will be so different.'

'Yes, that should put manners on some of them,' said James.

'Well, actually James,' said Don, 'I think you'll find that most people want that kind of clarity. Nobody enjoys ambiguity. Now, it may suit some people to hide behind confusion and use it as a defence mechanism for not doing things. Thankfully they are a minority though. But one thing is for sure, the business certainly doesn't need that vagueness,' he added.

'That's true,' said Clare. 'I know in my department, we certainly wouldn't get away with confusion regarding our numbers. The business wouldn't be able to function. So I suppose that should apply everywhere. And anyway, I agree. I've seen the frustration when people get mixed messages.'

Don continued, 'I believe that most people come to work wanting to do a good job. But a key part of that is giving them clarity on what's expected of them.'

'But they all have job descriptions, don't they?' asked James, looking to Clare.

'Yes, most of them do,' she answered. 'But in all honesty, no central repository exists and even if it did, they would surely be out of date. The business is changing all of the time and some of our people are here for years. Their jobs have changed significantly in that time,' she added.

'And because of that, there is ambiguity and confusion,' said Don. 'The confident ones just get on with it and do what they think their job entails. Let's call them the proactive ones. Then those who are less confident, or perhaps disengaged, just wait for direction. Let's call them the reactive ones. And what happens is that the reactors feel that the proactive ones are encroaching on their jobs. And the proactive ones classify the reactors as lazy. It's unnecessary confusion and it causes tension and silos,' he added.

'Does this go back to the point we discussed earlier about structure?' asked Clare.

'Yes it does,' said Don. 'As organisations keep busy with day-to-day operations and getting the job done, lines of accountability and responsibility can often get blurred. With the best of intentions, a structure may have been perfect at a point in time in the past. But then as the business matures and undoubtedly changes, people often make assumptions about who does what. Whereas in reality, the organisational chart needs to be revised.'

Clare then added, 'I suppose some will just get on and do things without realising they're crossing boundaries. Others may just abdicate responsibility and be quite happy for others to carry the load.'

Don added, 'One way or another, it can lead to tasks falling between stools, causing fatigue, errors and low morale. And that usually leads to poor business results.'

Leaving a pause for the point to sink in, Don continued, 'We also have to be careful about workload distribution. It can often happen that positive people are so engaged that they either volunteer for extra work or they get asked to do more.'

'Yes, I recognise that,' said Clare. 'The "willing horse" gets all the work. In my own team, Sophie always has her hand up first and is such a great girl. But then she takes on too much while others sit back.'

'While that's very admirable of Sophie, it can cause an imbalance, and potentially work the wrong way,' said Don.

'How do you mean?' asked James.

'Well, if Sophie has too much on already and is spread thinly, extra duties could result in nothing being done to the right standard or on time. On the other hand, there could be someone else on the team who is shyer about putting their hand up.'

'I hardly think a quiet person would be upset about not getting more work, surely?' said James.

'You might be surprised,' said Don. 'We just need to be mindful of workload distribution. There was a specific question related to this in the Workbly survey and the score indicated that it needs attention.

'Do you know, I'm beginning to see how all the values intertwine and impact on each other,' said Clare. 'We've already talked about "customer-first" and "respect". And I can see now how "accountability" links in with both of them.'

'That's exactly right,' said Don. 'We are working through them one at a time, but if only life was that simple!' he added.

'Well is it just a case of refreshing the job descriptions?' asked James.

'That is indeed part of it,' said Don. 'But let's back up a little first. Because what goes into the job descriptions is influenced by the direction you want to take the business. And that brings us back to the point I made earlier, budgets are not plans. Let me explain that a little more,' said Don as he invited James to take the wheel.

'Every year, around the time you are setting your budgets, it would serve you well to take time with your senior team to explore the bigger picture. Take a couple of days away off-site where you can collate various views around the table of what is going on in your market. That will enable you to make considered decisions about your long-term strategies. It will give you an opportunity to explore what changes you need to make regarding your people, your product mix, your route to market, your supply chain, systems and more. With that level of perspective, you may even find yourself using a zero-based approach to budgeting,' he added.

'What does that mean?' asked James.

'I suspect what Don is referring to is that we currently approach our next year's budget by taking a bottom-up approach rather than a top-down one. We review last year's numbers and add maybe 5 percent across the board. The alternative is to get a feel for the market and assess the opportunities and threats objectively. That might mean a higher target in some areas and a reduction in others. But overall, it grosses out a number that could even be higher than 5 percent. Is that it?' interjected Clare.

'That's it,' said Don. 'And in the straightforward "last year + 5 percent model", some people might be let off the hook for more ambitious targets. And some people get an increase in their budgets when perhaps their budgets should be cut.'

'Ah now, we're not that much of a soft touch,' said James very defensively.

'Of course we're not,' said Clare, 'but I do appreciate the spirit of the comment. We don't delve into the numbers enough. And when I look back particularly at the last two years, I think it might explain some of the reasons for our disappointing numbers.'

'How is that,' asked James. 'Perhaps if we had more strategic long-term conversations in the past, we'd have invested in our digital capabilities much sooner,' replied Clare. 'Our competitors beat us to it. And another example is our product portfolio. Undoubtedly we have some dogs in our range. Yet every year we add new lines and never seem to delist the slowest selling ones. We keep them in the range because maybe one customer buys them from us. But that adds to our cost base. It means we need more warehouse space, higher investment in stock and I honestly believe it sends a cluttered message to our customers,' she added.

Don encouraged a pause, as he performed his rice paper ritual.

'Budgets are not plans.'

Clare was on a roll and Don left her to make her excellent points. The debate continued and James was coming around more and more to this challenge to the status quo. He seemed to be a little less defensive, as the logic of the arguments were so convincing.

But before completely accepting everything, he asked, 'This is making sense, because I also know that sometimes we set conflicting targets. We give the sales guys an overall sales and margin target yet we give the marketing team a sales target for each product stream,' he added.

'Yes,' said Clare. 'That means that the sales guys care less about what they sell, as long as they hit their overall numbers. We'd be far better off getting both teams to somehow share a profit target. There'd be much less conflict,' she added.

'And another thing is that we also need to look at profit and loss analysis for each customer. I know for sure that we are servicing some customers at a loss,' said James. After a pause, he continued, 'But what does this have to with culture and how do we fit this with "accountability" as a value?' asked James.

'Once you have your big picture strategy fleshed out, that sets you up for the individual functions to develop sub-strategies for their own function – as a sub-set of the masterplan. The sales team should develop a detailed sales plan, as should the supply chain team for the supply chain, and of course that also applies to the bakery, marketing and so on. And the sum total of their plans and budgets adds up to the overall plan', said Don. 'That's the starting point for building accountability. The head of each function now owns a target that is relevant and appropriate to the overall strategy, which has been agreed by the whole team,' he added.

'But how does this change the culture, as it's not that far off what we have right now,' said James.

'Well it's only the start of it,' said Don. 'But don't underestimate the power of having this sort of clarity at this level and having it all documented and written down. In fairness, you didn't have this detail before. Budgets were set and function heads may or may not have signed off on them.'

Clare interjected 'That is definitely true, James. Our annual plans are predominantly a mixture of Excel spreadsheets.'

Don continued, 'I'm also suspicious that the leaders didn't share their own department plans with their peers in the senior team. What I'm proposing is that they cascade their plans and even involve their own teams in building their department plans. Doing that and sharing them with other depart-ments will make them accountable to their peers and their own teams.'

'So what you're saying is that by starting there, each plan has to be fully owned by that head of function and he or she has to then cascade that to each individual in their respective teams?' asked James.

'That's it,' said Don.

'And to their colleagues on the leadership team?' asked James.

'Yes,' said Clare.

'Now let's look at what metrics you tend to use,' said Don.

'They each have a set of key performance indicators that Clare develops,' said James. 'And it's a really good set of numbers that are done on sophisticated Excel reports, with pivot tables and the whole shooting gallery,' he added.

'They are for sure,' said Don. 'I've seen them. However I'd like to suggest that you also add in some softer measures, such as customer feedback scores and Workbly employee engagement scores. That will then ensure that people take the things that matter to the business for the long-term more seriously, not just a short-term horizon,' he added.

'That's a good idea,' added Clare. 'What gets measured gets done, so that allows us to put leadership behaviours into the mix. After all, you did say, Don, that "culture is about the way we do things around here"!'

CLONMACNOISE

Before closing off this part of the conversation, Don said, 'I know you have an "objectives" process where you give each leader individual objectives, in addition to their targets. You call them "personal objectives" but if you look closely, they tend to be departmental business objectives. Now I do understand that, but keep in mind that once we sign off on a new set of values or guiding principles, you'll want to ensure the leaders embrace them and take on board personal objectives linked to them.'

'That makes sense,' said James as he slowed the boat on the approach to Clonmacnoise jetty.

'And another point linked to your objective process, we need to be sure that the objectives are not just an extension of the day job activities.'

'I'm not sure I understand what you mean,' said Clare.

As they moored and locked up the boat, Don explained that objectives should be activities that are a quantum leap beyond the day job. 'Too often, objectives get mixed up with the day job,' said Don. 'For example, one of your sales director's objectives for last year was to deliver a 5 percent increase in sales in the retail channel. Now, I'd accept that if retail was a new channel for that year, but it wasn't. And another example was for your warehouse manager to improve service levels, but there was no metric attached. I'm sure you'll agree that the absence of a metric and a completion date is a "get out of jail free" card?'

As James and Clare indicated their agreement, Don excused himself and asked his guests to proceed on the tour without him. He said that he had some business matters to attend to and would need a few minutes to make some telephone calls.

With a look of concern, the Drinkwaters left without him. They took the short walk to the heritage centre and joined a guided tour that had just started. The highlight for them was the "Whispering Arch", an ornate gothic doorway built into the church. According to legend, they were told that the arch was used as a confessional, with the priests standing on the inside and the penitents whispering their sins through a recess on the outside.

James and Clare tried it out with James whispering something that caused Clare to giggle at first. Staying in position, he went on to make a promise about his relationship with the kids. It brought a tear to Clare's eyes that she hid from him.

In the meantime, Don made a couple of sensitive telephone calls. The last 24 hours had been very intense and exhausting and these calls were also challenging. They were time critical and necessary so he went below deck to avoid the wind noise.

When he finished his calls, Don once again went to work on the rice paper.

'Objectives without metrics (that include quality and quantity metrics, along with a timeframe) are a "get out of jail free" card.'

CLONMACNOISE TO BANAGHER

After the short tour of the settlement, James and Clare returned to the boat and they soon made haste for Banagher. As the journey got underway, they told Don about the tour. They marvelled at the ancient architecture and the logic behind building a round tower, with its door reachable only with a ladder.

Don said, 'Can we chat about how to make people more accountable in meetings?'

He asked his guests to describe again the format for their meetings. He had gotten some feedback already of course but wanted James to volunteer the structure himself. Don felt it would be better if James himself acknowledged the opportunity for improvement, rather than Don telling him.

Using a classic coaching skill, he asked, 'James, in the spirit of improved accountability, how do you think those meetings could improve?'

'Well I think we should at the very least make sure that for every topic we discuss, we should agree an action and document it,' he said.

'Not only that, said Clare, 'but we should allocate an owner to each action.'

'Now you're talking Clare,' said James. 'And don't worry, I don't mean that in a "gotcha" way, but it would just be so clear for everyone' he added.

'Following on from that,' said Don. 'Can we make sure that in each subsequent meeting, you revisit the actions agreed at the previous one? After the first couple of meetings like that, your team will get the message fast and furiously that you mean business and that you are holding activity-owners to account. And of course we should tell them that you'd like them to use the same new format at their own team meetings too,' he added.

'Consider this,' Don continued. 'Wouldn't it be great if every meeting was to begin with a clear agenda, outlining the objective of the meeting. And then for it to end with a detailed list of actions. Before closing the meeting, use RACI with each action.'

'I've heard of RACI before,' said Clare. 'Remind me again?'

'"R" determines who is "responsible" for a particular activity, in other words the person or persons doing the job. "A" is for who is "accountable", that means the "buck stops here" which will only ever be one person. Who should be "consulted" for their input before signoff is "C" and for those who should be kept in the loop and at least "informed" about it, they get added to the "I" list.'

'That's a bit heavy, don't you think?' said James. 'I guess it is when you hear it at first,' said Don. 'But you'd be surprised at how people appreciate it and get used to it very quickly. You'll actually find that after a while, people will start coming to meetings having thought about RACI in advance. Not only does it achieve better accountability but it also pays respect to those not directly involved.'

'There we go again,' said Clare. 'You can see how all the values interconnect and are co-dependent on each other. But tell me Don, is there a risk that we'd be seen to be micro-managing if we went into that detail?'

Don answered 'Not necessarily, Clare. You see that depends on the level of detail you get into in the meetings. With leaders, you have to assume that they know the big picture and how to get the job done. After all, that's why they are leaders.'

'That's true,' said Clare. Don continued, 'The micro-managing comes in to play when leaders literally micro-manage their people. That means watching over their shoulder at every turn and dare I say it, being a pain in the ass!' he laughed.

'That is something we need to be careful of,' said Clare. 'Because I know if I was being micro-managed, then I'd probably find myself deferring decision-making to my boss and not taking responsibility myself.'

Don told them the story of another client project that he was involved in. The VP of Sales, in consultation with his boss, the CEO, carved up the Canada region into nine sales territories. Sometime later in Ontario, two of their biggest competitors announced a merger. In the weeks that followed, there was a board meeting and this merger was never even discussed at it. It turned out that the VP of Sales didn't even know about it, despite the fact that his Ontario team was in a quandary about it.

'Well,' said James on hearing that story, 'that VP should have known. He is not being accountable.'

Don continued 'It actually gets worse. That same VP is a micro-manager. He knows exactly when his direct reports haven't submitted their vacation requests on time and he chases them forensically about their personal expenses.'

'Wow, how does he still have a job?' asked Clare.

As they travelled the meandering river, they observed the ancient bogland on both sides of the river. This prompted Don to tell more stories of the Mystical Waterway, Ireland's Ancient East and Hidden Heartlands. 'The Irish Tourist Board has done a great job developing and promoting these destinations. The reason for developing them was to attract tourists to all parts of the country and not just the well-known centres like Dublin and Killarney. That's why the culturally aware tourists come here. And of course when the authority engaged with the local stakeholders and explained *why* they were doing this, they all bought into it,' he added.

'Speaking of *why*, that reminds me,' Don continued. 'Be mindful too to always explain "why" things are being done. Context is so important for improved understanding which increases commitment to act. I promise, all of this helps motivation and morale and it speeds up execution of whatever has been agreed.'

'And what if someone was to just rock up to a meeting without having done what they previously signed up to do?' asked James. 'In this new spirit of mollycoddling, I'm assuming that I can't say a word?' he laughed.

'Now come on James, you know very well that is not what Don is saying.'

'Of course I do,' he smiled as if he just couldn't help himself, 'but tell me.'

As they passed the mooring at Shannonbridge and slowed to under 5 km per hour, Don continued, 'Let's consider rewards and consequences. There is a conversation to be had about your bonus structure. I suggest we don't get into the detail for now as it's a big conversation and probably an emotive one. My reason for alluding to it now is that I don't think your incentives are strong enough.'

'What?' exclaimed James. 'But we pay out a lot on bonuses!'

'When you calculate the maximum a leader can earn in bonus and then the net amount after tax, I wouldn't be surprised if they thought it wasn't worth the extra effort. So they'll do just enough to keep you off their back, and no more.'

'But our bonus budget is huge, Don,' said James.

'Yes it is,' said Don. 'But people come to expect it as part of their salary. Because the metrics are sometimes dubious, it just turns into a row each year and you usually give in so as not to lose a good person.'

'So what are you saying, we need to allocate more money to it?' asked James.

'Not necessarily, but possibly yes,' said Don. 'But you link the increased bonus to targets that are challenging, yet achievable with a stretch. People may join the public sector to work for lots of reasons, one of them is security and certainty of income. But on the other hand, people often join the private sector to embrace the excitement of performance-related reward,' he added.

'I think that could work James, from a financial perspective,' said Clare. 'It makes sense to me. It should be self-financing. But Don, what about the flip side of all this? Should there be consequences for not hitting targets or is that creating a negative fearful culture?'

'Look, guys,' said Don. 'You are not a vindictive organisation. It's not your style to deliberately treat people badly and to go around looking for victims to fire. However, in this age of rising costs and fierce competition, both in the physical world and online, every organisation has to be more disciplined about its return on investment. Rewards and consequences play a part in that. That's just the way it is,' he said.

Don continued, 'One of my retail clients has hundreds of departments across its estate of stores. And therefore it has hundreds of managers. We managed to introduce a culture in the organisation where every department manager treated his or her department as if it was their own store. We encouraged that strongly. They were expected to know their targets, their best and worst sellers and when new product was coming in. They had profit and loss visibility and they were fully accountable for what went on in their department. And they were paid accordingly, with good bonuses linked to performance.'

'But did that not lead to anarchy and fierce internal competition?' asked James.

'It certainly bred a competitive spirit,' said Don. 'But not to the point that they didn't work together to give great customer experiences. There were rules and they had to comply and operate within guidelines. And of course there were different targets for each department. Those targets were a combination of hard profit and loss targets and softer ones to do with customer service and team engagement. Their bonus was also influenced by their behaviours, which were of course linked to the company values.'

Don continued, 'I know of one occasion with that client, where a particular salesperson gave a bad experience to a customer. The customer gave a damning review in the next survey, causing that department to get a very poor score in that month. Consequently the whole team missed their monthly target and no individual got their monthly bonus. The offender was mortified and went around to each of her colleagues – and apologised to each one individually. That's accountability,' said Don. He went on to articulate other examples, some that included famous politicians who "fell on their swords" and had to resign from their positions in disgrace.

'I'm wondering about other ways to reward our people Don, without it involving money all the time,' said Clare.

'Well Clare,' said Don, 'You are bang on the button there. Recognition is a powerful motivator too. There is so much research already done in this field that proves that money is not the most important driver.'

'Continue!' said James with a droll voice and a smile that didn't at all surprise Clare and Don.

'Recognising effort and/or achievement by thanking or acknowledging people is extraordinarily effective. Letting them know that you appreciate their efforts is so basic and yet so impactful. And before you say it,' laughed Don. 'Yes I know people are just doing their job. But far too often managers only point out the things that are wrong, which is not balanced or fair,' he added. 'Those managers are missing a very simple trick.'

Clare continued, 'Do you know, we have situations where managers have even taken credit for ideas that I know well have come from a member of their team. And it really bothers me.'

'I'm sorry to say,' said Don, 'that phenomenon occurs more frequently than you think. It tells a lot about that manager's character. They are showing that their leadership positioning is still at a basic entry-level stage, that is, leadership linked to position or title. They are putting their ego before their own teams. If they were at the pinnacle of leadership, they would not be in competition with their own team members.'

'In contrast,' he continued. 'Let me tell you about Henry Ward, the CEO of a software company called Carta. During Covid-19, it was decided that 10 percent of the workforce of 161 would have to be let go. In an announcement to his company, he said that the decision was entirely his and asked people not to blame their managers. This is an example of being fully accountable. "The buck stops here",' said Don.

'I can see we have a lot to do here,' said James. 'You see I think we got spoiled in the previous five years by the growth we had, without much effort. We probably didn't have to be so structured and precise. We had a rhythm going and people just got on with it,' he added.

'I agree,' said Clare. 'But those days are gone now that the world has experienced such disruption, with Covid-19, etc. We, just like every other business, have to be more careful about our costs.'

'Yes, more accountable,' added James.

BANAGHER

As they approached Banagher marina, James made some positive remarks about the cleanliness of the place, the beautiful environment and then added, 'Bloody heck, I've never seen so many cows in one field!'

That brought the conversation around to greenhouse gases and the general environment. 'Just so you know,' said James. 'We started a Corporate Social Responsibility programme two years ago and it really resonated with our customers and employees. I'm happy that we have shown that we care about the circular economy. We have stepped up our recycling internally and all company vehicles will be electric inside three years,' he added.

'That's wonderful,' said Don. 'So you're being accountable as an organisation too. Well done!'

James moored the boat like a professional, while Don and Clare did what they had to do with the ropes. When they finished, Don went to work again with his rice paper.

'Reward and consequences are essential enablers of accountability.'

7

AGILITY

Overnight in Banagher

Don surprised his guests when he said, 'You'll be staying tonight in a beautiful B&B called Charlotte's Way, which is closely linked to an iconic Englishwoman.'

'Ah, Charlotte Rampling,' said James.

'Nope, try again and this time think of Jane Eyre,' said Don.

'It's Charlotte Brontë,' said Clare.

Don nodded and said, 'The house itself is nearly 300 years old but apparently Charlotte's husband, Arthur Nicholls, moved here after her death in 1855.'

'Isn't it an amazing coincidence,' said Clare, 'that the central theme running through her famous novel, *Jane Eyre*, is about values such as self-respect and self-truth. Jane is not willing to compromise her values even for those things she wants most.'

'Bloody heck Don, I have to compliment you on your attention to detail. Did you actually plan this?' asked James.

Don just laughed and said nothing. He himself was quite shocked at the unplanned connection. He had never read *Jane Eyre* or seen the film but he certainly had planned the itinerary. He wanted to perform another rice-paper ritual that said *'You make your own luck'* but decided instead to keep that little nugget to himself.

'Let me tell you my plan, and see if you're happy with it. Let's go to the B&B. You can check in and freshen up then I suggest we come back here to

72

the boat. Banagher is a small town and there isn't much choice for food so how would you feel about getting a light takeaway delivered to us?'

'That's a great idea,' said Clare. 'We've had a lot to eat already today.' James agreed so they packed up and started walking.

After ten paces, Don's phone vibrated in his pocket. He excused himself and asked his guests to continue without him. He asked them to wait for him outside J.J. Hough's.

'Where is that?' asked James.

'Don't worry, you won't miss it.'

Somewhat bemused and bewildered, James and Clare walked up the gentle gradient of the town's main street. Banagher is a very quiet town that has two main attractions. One is that it has a very modern marina. The other is that it's the home of a famous singing pub called J.J. Hough's, one of the top 20 pubs in Ireland. They reached a premises on their left that can only be described as an urban forest that sells beer. With aluminium kegs outside the door and an abundance of creeper covering the old shopfront, and little else to catch their eye, they knew they had arrived at J.J. Hough's.

Don caught up with them and they continued the walk to the B&B. Don helped them to check in and after taking their takeaway order he told them he'd see them back at the boat.

When they were all settled back on the boat facing into the setting sun, James and Clare expressed their surprise at how quiet the town was. Don told them that there was a time when Banagher was a main crossing point between Connacht and Leinster and was the centre of trade. 'Many years ago on market days, the horses would be lined up on both sides of the town and stretch for over three kilometres,' said Don.

'That's two miles to a Brexiteer,' he laughed as he looked at James. 'The market was so famous across Europe that it even attracted buyers on behalf of the Italian and Russian governments.'

They chatted some more about olden times and what it must have been like to live in that era. They contrasted with the world of today and how much the world keeps changing.

'You cannot stop change,' said Don as he opened a bottle of Malbec.

'Banagher is just one real example of how the sands of time keep shifting everything, everywhere and everyone,' he added. 'You know it wasn't that long before Charlotte Brontë wrote her famous novel that the modern workplace as we know it commenced. Three hundred years ago there were no such things as offices or factories. Most people probably worked on the land or in their homes and everything was measured in outputs. In other words:

what and how much they produced. Then one of the first office environments was opened in London by the East India Company, where workers attended on a daily basis.'

While sipping his Malbec and with the onset of hunger, James snapped back, 'Here we go. Don you're treading on thin ice now giving me a British history lesson.'

Don laughed but continued, 'With that new work style and centralised environment came a new way of measuring productivity by inputs. In other words what you do and what hours you worked. The recent lockdown has changed that for many who are working now from home. Bosses now have to trust that their teams are putting in the hours. Or more importantly, that they're getting the work done to the right standard and on time. It brings accountability to the fore!'

'Don that's enough bloody history!' laughed James.

'I'm saying this for a reason,' said Don. 'Look, we all know how the world continues to change. I'm not just referring to the fallout of the pandemic by the way. We were already experiencing exponential growth in the speed, the volume and the complexity of change.'

'Well that's for sure,' said Clare. 'Brexit was the big story before Covid-19, as was the dramatic shift in the balance of trade with China and the rest of the world, for example.'

'Yes, you're right,' added James. 'Look at what went on with Donald Trump's administration and the increase in tariffs between the US and China. The list just goes on and on, doesn't it?'

'We're seeing it too in our own business,' said Clare. 'Look at how diets are changing with people's increasing concern for health and wellness. Look at how the green agenda is gathering even more steam, and all for the good I should add.'

'Yes and look at how we're getting our asses kicked by some of our competitors,' said James with a sulk, 'and the ongoing investment required for even more IT.' As he said that, he went a little quiet, as he thought once again of the differences he has had with his son Tom about changes he wanted to introduce.

Dinner on Board

The food arrived and they tucked in to pizzas from Gianni's takeaway. It was a pleasant balmy evening and they sat on deck around the table. There was a nice family atmosphere in the marina with lots of people gathered on each other's boats and kids running around laughing.

'Many of our customers are really bothered by AirBnB,' said Clare.

'I'm not surprised,' said Don. 'They are the Amazon of the hospitality sector and are really shaking up the industry.'

'Yes,' said James. 'But they offer a totally different customer experience and they are no competition for some of our hospitality customers.'

'I'm not so sure about that,' said Clare. 'Just like with any of the disruptors, such as Netflix, Uber and Amazon, I think they observed from afar that their target industries were perhaps complacent, and decided to challenge the status quo by exploiting mobile technology.'

'That is true,' said Don. 'But, of course your hotel customers can't just roll over and give in to them. In the same way that good retailers have identified the gaps in Amazon's customer experience, so too can your hotel customers. After all, they can't compete directly with the global might of these digital disruptors. But they can certainly fight local battles that they know they can win.'

'But how can they do that?' asked James. 'Traditional hotels are at such a price disadvantage with AirBnB that they could never compete. Not to mention the exorbitant fees that the online bookers charge that eat into their margins. I really feel for the hotels in this mad world.'

'I do too,' said Don. 'Let me give you an example. Here in Ireland, the so-called German discount retailers arrived here a number of years ago. Just like the Vikings, they caused havoc with traditional grocery retailers like Dunnes, Supervalu and Eurospar. The Irish companies could never compete on price, due to the scale that the Germans have. So they exploited other advantages they had, such as wider product ranges, branded goods, customer service and store ambience.'

'And was that enough for them Don?' asked Clare.

'There is no doubt that Aldi and Lidl made inroads and secured significant market share,' said Don. 'But the legacy businesses are still thriving and still dominate the overall mix. It proves to me once again that price has a role but is not the be-all and end-all for customers.'

'How did they do that?' asked James. 'They adapted,' said Don. 'They moved fast; they collaborated with their suppliers; they reformatted stores; and they refreshed their messaging. They did all that with great pace and agility. And that, my dear friends, brings me to the fourth value or guiding principle.' Don said one word, 'agility,' as he did his ritual on rice paper.

'Digital disruptors change the dynamic in an industry.
You can embrace it or ignore it. Coping with it is up to you.'

'I believe there are opportunities too for GTD to be more agile, so as to maintain relevance with your customers. But I have to tell you that it will require some more change.'

'What are you referring to Don?' asked James.

'Well, let me first of all acknowledge that you have made two significant changes in recent times. You added the bakery and you invested in an online platform.'

'We certainly did,' said James. 'And the bakery was the best idea ever,' he added, proudly.

But, of course the bakery was James' own idea, although it took four years from incubation of the idea to execution. He had resisted the investment in IT initially. Consequently, GTD was much later coming to that party than was good for them.

'That's totally correct James,' said Don.

'There's a "but' coming, I can feel it,' laughed James.

'Well, there is an inconsistency across the various teams,' said Don. 'The bakery guys are quite progressive and they get frustrated with the warehouse and delivery teams. In fact, they actually told me that they'd be really happy if they were split out from the wider business and had their own sales and marketing, to complete their end-to-end system.'

'Well I can tell you,' said James, 'that's not going to happen. If we did that, the core business would have less of a differentiator and remember you mentioned the importance of relevance to customers? They need each other. Why don't they see that?'

Don replied, "Now by the way, I'm not commenting on whether that is a good idea or not, that's a question to be raised when we come to strategy and structure. But right now, it's causing friction."

Don continued, 'I get a sense of lethargy and stagnation around the business. We already talked about accountability and silos earlier, so I won't repeat those issues. But more than that, I get a sense that teams are treading water. The machine that is the day-to-day business is quite well-oiled. But there is something missing for me. And I'll sum it up with the word "pace". Or to widen it a bit more, it's "agility,"' he added.

'Do you mean we need to crack the whip some more?' asked James with a smirk.

Clare ignored the comment and said, 'I read a lot throughout the lockdown about "agile" organisations, how they work differently and are able to adapt to change really quickly. I also saw a report that showed that companies with a recognised "agile" culture re-emerged from the previous global financial crisis faster than their peers,' she added.

'Yes,' said Don. 'I too came across a number of really good examples. A US-based retailer that launched kerbside delivery in two days, during the lockdown, versus the previously planned eighteen months. An engineering company here in Ireland took just one week to switch the regular production of their widgets to the design and manufacture of ventilators. And a global telco redeployed and trained 1,000 of its store-based employees to a contact centre sales department in three weeks. The list of fantastic Covid-19 lockdown examples of agility goes on and on.'

'I suppose what the pandemic proved is that when the chips are down, fast decisions can be made. So we should make it the norm,' said James. 'I know that the word "agile" means to be nimble and probably flexible too. But what does it mean in organisational culture?'

Don explained, 'The word "agile" was introduced with fanfare in the software industry in 2001. Prior to that there was a culture in that sector of "loner-coders" who tended to work alone with slow and bureaucratic decision-making. Then some of the leading industry players came together for a retreat and came out the other side with what they called *The Agile Manifesto*. In simple terms, it was a redesign of how software would be developed using teams and short-term projects.'

As he poured some more wine, Don loosely referred to the website *agilemanifesto.org* and described how the founders have come to value individuals and interactions over processes and tools; working software over comprehensive documentation; customer collaboration over contract negotiation; and they prefer to respond to change over following a plan.

'But Don, we don't develop software. We sell food. What has that got to do with us?' asked James.

'Yes of course,' said Clare. 'But I'm sure what he means is that the principles can be applied across other parts of our business.'

'That's it exactly Clare,' said Don. 'The lockdown in particular caused many companies to remove obstacles, bureaucracies and boundaries to enable fast decision-making. Some have broken down silos and got people working together in ways no one ever thought was possible. As with the *Agile Manifesto*, they found that by putting the right people in the room with the right mix of skills – and with a very short burst of time, productivity increased. Decisions and processes were streamlined and frontline people were empowered.'

'I'm just not sure,' said James. 'Our industry is quite static. We have an annual budgeting cycle. Our customers' business is seasonal and the cycles are quite predictable. We have to be careful.'

'Yes,' said Don. 'But we're not talking about a complete transformation here. The software industry is indeed very different and the speed of change there is scary. But that's not to say that your industry is not changing. It is, as we discussed earlier. My concern is that if you don't embrace some of the same principles and introduce more urgency, the lethargy that I mentioned will prevail. And that will be to your detriment.'

'What are we talking about then? I mean, what's involved?' asked James. 'Look James, as with the other values, we're not making hard decisions yet. So let's keep chatting here and just brainstorm. Is that okay? But let me give you an example of a bureaucratic organisation whose culture is the polar opposite of agile.'

As he cleared up after the meal, Don continued, 'In the world of international fashion, buyers need to have flexibility to travel to the four corners of the world to meet suppliers. One case I'm familiar with is a multi-billion-euro company that sources merchandise from all over the world. Yet the buyers are not allowed to book airline tickets until they get approval from the CEO. Consequently, they often don't get to travel, or, if they do, they find themselves booking tickets at the last minute. So they end up paying top dollar for those tickets or perhaps just not going at all.'

'That's another example of micro-managing,' said Clare.

'It is for sure,' said Don. 'But it's also an example of a slow-moving company. What should happen is that the buyers be given a travel budget and be made accountable for that. But the CEO doesn't trust the team and makes it difficult for them.'

As James nodded in agreement, Don continued. 'One of the big changes in an agile culture is to introduce *task forces*. They are a mix of relevant people from across the business that work on a defined project for a defined period of time.'

Clare added, 'I assume you know that we did have them when developing the bakery idea and when installing the new online platform?'

'I do,' said Don. 'But I'm sure you'll agree that both projects could have been expedited more quickly. We also know about the resistance, the noise and the bad feeling, particularly with the IT project.'

'I think much of that was to do with the way they were set up,' said Clare. 'Planning wasn't good and the teams couldn't make decisions because we micro-managed it. And our Tom was on that IT project.' That comment introduced a moment of awkwardness as James just stared at his glass.

'Let me give you an example,' said Don. 'I was working with a large retailer that is a global icon in its industry. This company continues to win awards and deliver financial results that beat all records. If I was held up against a wall and had to describe its culture in one sentence, I'd say this. Within its leadership, there is a very high level of dissatisfaction, with everything.'

'Gosh,' said Clare. 'That sounds like a nightmare place to work. Are they ever satisfied?'

'Well it's certainly not for the faint-hearted, that's for sure,' said Don. 'But they see themselves as a premier retailer on the global stage with lots of aggressive competition around them. This culture is part of what they see as their differentiator. Just because something worked last year, or just because something has been done a certain way for a number of prior years, is no guarantee that they'll do it again in the future.'

Don continued, 'You know the expression, "if it ain't broken then don't fix it"?' Before James or Clare could answer, he added, 'this company believes that "if it ain't broken, then go ahead and break it". That "can-do" and proactive mindset is what drives them on to keep trying new things. By the way, they also put "customer" at the heart of all they do and every single person is accountable for their actions. And I should add that innovation is highly valued too.'

'It all sounds exhausting,' said Clare.

'There is no doubt, Clare, that it's a fast-moving organisation,' said Don. 'But this level of agility is actually rewarding and highly motivational. I suspect that in your new breakneck world, you don't have a choice in GTD either.'

'Don, don't forget that our business is very traditional. We buy and sell stuff. That's it!' said James. 'I appreciate that trying new things, like we did with the bakery, is very important. But when you talk about innovation, I tend to think of technology more than anything else.'

'I do understand that,' said Don. 'But I want you to see it as a way of life in other parts of your business too. Because of the speed of change, innovation is essential for every organisation in every industry. And the culture needs to enable an environment where it is encouraged, but not in a reckless or sloppy way.'

Don let that point settle and then continued, 'I'm a big fan of collaboration, especially when it is safe and appropriate to do so. But be careful, collaboration without honesty and structure can lead to poor consensus. And poor consensus should not be an excuse for bad judgement. One person has to make a decision and be accountable at the end of the day.'

'And there we are, back around to "accountability",' added Clare.

'I have met organisations with a so-called "blame culture",' said Don 'where it is safer to keep your head down than to try new things and risk failure. People feel that they are witch-hunted for getting it wrong. For one company that I'm familiar with, key executives get physically sick or don't sleep the night before a big meeting. They dread and fear the wrath of a bullying boss who exposes them for failing with a new product or for trying something new.'

'Well clearly, that is shocking,' said James. 'That culture would impede growth and the organisation would lose out in the long run. In saying that however, it's not fair to expect an organisation to just turn a blind eye to failure when significant funds go down the drain, not to mention the time wasted. So what's the right balance, Don?'

Don went on to give an overview for how innovation should be managed.

'Start by encouraging innovation, but not without structure. Leaders ought to encourage creativity and innovation, then reward and recognise outcomes. But they should make it very clear in advance, what the criteria for success are. Then the individuals involved should apply rigorous project management disciplines to their concepts. Lack of structure can lead to too much subjectivity and not enough objectivity.'

'I like the idea of it being organised,' said James. 'I wouldn't be a fan of madcap ideas that cause a distraction!'

'Yes,' said Don. 'But you can make it safe to fail without accepting incompetence. It's totally appropriate and reasonable for innovation to be encouraged. But it's not realistic for individuals to be sloppy and wasteful, and not get called out on that. As with all things in life, there is a need for balance here. Whether it's a success or a failure, discuss it openly and learn from it.'

'That is something we don't do enough of, James. We don't review and learn. In fact we've even repeated mistakes of the past, I hate to admit,' commented Clare.

Don continued, 'Even when applying rigour as I've just described, not every idea will work out as expected.'

'How can we apply all of this in GTD?' asked Clare. 'What changes do we have to make?'

'Task forces are just one characteristic of an agile culture,' said Don. 'They're not the only one. Nevertheless, let's talk about them to help bring the concept to life. There are a number of applications where task forces would be appropriate.'

'I know of one already,' said James. 'I'd like to explore some new product categories for the business. I have lots of ideas for the bakery ranges and for our core range that require more innovation. Would that be appropriate?'

'Absolutely,' said Don. 'That's a perfect example.'

Then Clare added, 'Another idea is to take the discussion we had earlier about customer-centricity. Wouldn't a task force work for that too, to see how we can really put customers at the heart of all decision-making across all touchpoints in our business?'

'Both of those are perfect examples. And you can add others to that too, such as planning for Brexit, or supply chain efficiencies that will remove your dependence on having only one source in the Far East for your bakery ingredients. The list goes on,' said Don.

'So what makes a good task force?' asked James.

'I'll keep this brief for now,' said Don. 'We've covered a lot today and I'm sure you must be tired of my voice by now. Once you pick a topic, you decide at a broad level what and why you want this. Then you invite a number of people with a mix of skills and from across the business to join the team.'

'What's the ideal size team?' asked Clare.

'Well, there isn't one,' said Don. 'It depends on the project but I'd say possibly between five and nine. Your brief to them needs to be very clear and give them a fixed timeframe to develop a plan. Whether you can expect them to deliver it once again depends on the project. But you have to empower them and enable them to get on with it.'

'Don you mentioned the word collaboration earlier, even with regard to competitors. Do you mean that?' asked Clare.

'I do Clare,' replied Don. 'You see competitiveness is both a positive trait and potentially a negative one. It can prevent you seeing opportunities that might be staring you in the face. For example, how crazy would it be for you to collaborate with competitors when sourcing your ingredients or raw materials? You might increase your buying power. Or how crazy would it be to collaborate on outbound logistics? You have trucks on the road that are half-empty, despite your best efforts in planning routes and scheduling.'

'Mm, that's probably going too far,' said James.

'Yes I do understand your reticence James. And perhaps it is. But I want to open your mind to the possibilities of more creative collaboration,' said Don.

'And that could also include bringing customers into a task force. After all, you do that already in your industrial kitchen by inviting chefs in to test new ingredients and recipes. What about developing an internal team along with some key customers, to explore ways to help them sell more product?' he added.

Clare said, 'I do think we should be open to it and look at it sooner rather than later.'

'Now of course,' said Don, 'you can also see how "agility" links with "respect" and "accountability". You don't just let the task force loose without parameters. That doesn't mean you micro-manage them,' he laughed. 'But I think you should let them come up with their own parameters. That'll show them respect and you'll find that they themselves will want to be account-able too.'

'I like that,' said Clare.

Don continued 'Give them say six weeks and encourage them to innovate and think like a start-up, not a legacy business that's been around for years. That incubates a truly entrepreneurial spirit that is infectious and a great trait to have, even as a business matures. After all, you'd never hear a start-up saying "this is the way we've always done it"!'

'And do we just stand back and leave them to it, and let them sell the family silver?' asked James with a little concern in his voice.

'Nope,' said Don. 'That's where the parameters come in. And as well as that, I'll work with them using a tried and tested structured approach for the first one. Your job is to be supportive and available if and when you're needed.'

'I'm happy to take the lead on that James,' said Clare.

Don went on, 'But given that we want to instil a sense of urgency, it may be a case of you accepting 80 percent and then pressing "Go" with their recommendations. In other words, to seek total perfection is probably not the answer. Perfection is the enemy of getting things done. Or as Dr Mike Ryan, the Executive Director of the World Health Organization Health Emergencies Programme, said about developing a new vaccine for Covid-19, "perfect should not bully the good".'

'I guess that's why we get frequent version updates on our smartphone apps,' said James.

'After the first task force,' said Clare. 'What comes next?'

'Well, let's assume the project is a success, you need to extract and share the learning so that it can be repeated again and again. It also brings that stage of the project to a formal close. That does a number of things. It ensures accountability as we discussed earlier. It also gives you an opportunity to formally recognise or reward the team members and to celebrate the success. And no James, before you say a word,' laughed Don. 'That's not mollycoddling. That's just good business sense.'

James smiled, thought for a moment and said, 'You know orchestras always play to a defined score. And that's okay. But I'm sure you've heard of the famous jazz musician Duke Ellington. He used to encourage and empower his band members to experiment and try new riffs. They had a fabulous sound and were really successful.'

With that perfectly timed cue, Don said, 'Banagher has its own version of Duke Ellington and any other talented musician in the world that you can imagine. Let's go and pop in to J.J. Hough's for a nightcap. And just so you know, we won't be chatting in there. So we'll continue this in the morning.'

As they readied themselves to walk up the main street, Don reassured them that while this concept is new to them, it's being used by many of the great and the good to wonderful effect. Once again he reminded them that a task force is just one example of agility. He outlined other examples, such as coping in a crisis with agility, dealing with unexpected or emerging challenges with urgency, supporting the new trend for home-working and also being flexible with workforce numbers to suit seasonal demands. 'There are so many ways to bring "agile" to life and we'll talk about those in more detail at the planning stage.'

'Yes,' said Clare. 'I think when we put the challenge to the team and explain where we're going with all of this and, of course why, I have no doubt that they will embrace it and have some great ideas.'

Don added, 'If having a high level of dissatisfaction with everything is a step too far, it'd be great if we can at least pick up the pace and create a constant sense of urgency.'

'Would that not be too frenetic and cause a perpetual state of stress?' asked Clare.

'I guess,' said Don, 'it's all about balance. We need to weave it in with "accountability" and "respect" at the same time.'

He continued, 'Having one agile team is great, but having several across the business will make the whole boat go faster. Some sacred cows might be challenged along the way. We can tap into the collective intelligence, wisdom and goodwill of your great teams.'

'Yes,' said James. 'In fairness, we do have some good teams.'

'But, of course, they'll need the right structure and support,' said Don.

'Agility on its own is unsafe without the other values to counter-balance it. And it also requires an adjustment in leadership style. And that starts at the top,' he said, as he tapped James on the back.

Don knew that he was on safe ground making such a comment. James had clearly turned a corner and had shifted his thinking quite a bit. Don was impressed with him, after all James is in his fifties and has built up a personal and leadership style in that time, with lots of good, and not so good, habits.

The issue with Sarah and Tom is still hanging there nevertheless. And that is where this could succeed or unravel, he thought. But he was working on a plan and had just a few more moves to make before he could declare a win-win.

After a couple of hours of "craic agus ceol", where no words can match the real-life experience of a visit to J.J. Hough's, James, Clare and Don bid each other goodnight. James and Clare turned left and headed to the B&B. Don turned right and returned to his boat. Before retiring, he reached for a hazelnut, the edible ink pen and a piece of rice paper.

'The volume, the complexity and the speed of change demands an agile culture, otherwise you get left behind.'

8

WRAPPING IT ALL UP

Return Journey on the Final Day

James and Clare woke to an array of agricultural sounds that included a distant tractor and cows being herded home for their morning milking by a barking collie. It was another sunny day with a gentle breeze blowing the curtains. Clare looked out the window to enjoy the beautiful flowers in the front gardens and, to her right, the nearby imposing church steeple.

Over breakfast, they chatted about what they had learned so far. They both shared their satisfaction with what they discovered, despite the occasional negative issue. But they reminded themselves of Don's reassurance that there was nothing that wasn't fixable with the right attitude and application.

Clare checked and rechecked that James was genuinely on-board with it all. He did of course have concerns, but they were more about managing the change than whether the changes were required in the first place. Clare was really pleased that he had made this transformation but she also acknowledged that she was somewhat scared about the task ahead of them.

'I have to be honest Clare, I was starting to feel overwhelmed with it all and quite daunted by how much is involved', said James. 'But I couldn't sleep last night thinking about it all. And I'm actually looking forward to getting back to it now. I can see what Don means about it being fixable. It just needs to be carefully planned.'

'Me too,' said Clare. 'I was full sure that Don's discovery would perhaps highlight a few issues around processes and I was even expecting some challenges around structure. But that feedback from the customers bothered me. I'm amazed at how accurate it is. In all honesty James, we couldn't argue even one issue. And let's remind ourselves that the feedback came from customers and our own people. Don just drew insights from it all.'

'He did,' said James. 'But even the insights make perfect sense. I realise now that if we were to just try to fix the issues one at a time, it would be like a band-aid on an ulcer. They'd be short-term fixes only. If we want this to have long-term impact and for us to create our legacy we need to go to the root of them all and address the culture.'

'I couldn't agree more,' said Clare. 'And if we have any hope of getting Tom and Sarah back involved, we have to commit to whatever changes we make. That could be our legacy.'

James said, 'Look Clare. This trip has been an epiphany for me. I realise that I've been stubborn and self-righteous. It's not that long ago since we took over the business from my father. And remember what that was like? It was as if he was losing a limb and it nearly drove us both to emigrate to Australia.'

'I remember it well,' said Clare. 'That was a very difficult time, but we got through it. But let's not repeat that for our kids. Surely we can learn from that?'

'Yes we can, Clare,' said James. 'I promise that I'm determined to embrace this. I just didn't appreciate the impact of my own actions up to now and I feel a little emotional about it all, to be honest. I can't wait to have a good heart-to-heart with Tom and Sarah. I want to explain what I'm thinking right now. I don't mean to excuse anything, but just let them see that I want to move on with them, not without them.' Clare just smiled and gave him a hug.

He continued, 'I guess we have been so busy growing the business and doing the day job, I couldn't see the wood for the trees. That's what has made this time out with Don so effective. But I do have concerns.'

'Why don't we make a list of our concerns now before we see Don and then chat about them as we make our way further south to Portumna?' said Clare.

'That's a good idea,' said James as they packed up their bags.

Clare took out a notepad and started the list, 'I'll start the list with "what are the next steps?"'

James added one of his own, 'How long will this take?'

Clare added two more, 'Who will be involved and what do you and I have to do? What's our role?'

'Yes,' said James. 'I'm really curious about that too. And I'd also like to know how much disruption it'll cause and if there are any risks. After all, we won't be able to do everything. This will all have to be phased.'

Clare thought of one more question, 'How will we overcome the inevitable resistance and cynicism we'll get, apart from firing everyone?' she laughed. James laughed too at the joke that was clearly referring to him.

As they walked, James expressed remorse for what he called his stupidity in how he let his relationship with Tom and Sarah deteriorate. 'Clare I know you've been trying to tell me for a long time and I just wasn't listening. I know you've been caught in some very stressful situations in trying to keep the peace. I feel very bad about that and I so want to address it. I just wish they were here now today so we could talk about it and put it right. But I know they'd be highly suspicious of me and just think I had been smoking some Irish shamrock over the last few days,' he said with a nervous laugh.

'I do too,' said Clare. 'But they're both doing their thing and we won't see them for another ten days when they come to us for your birthday dinner. But if I know Sarah, she'll be very warm to the idea of having a chat. Tom will be a greater challenge as he feels very hurt about being undermined in front of the team.'

'Yes Clare, I know exactly what he's referring to. There were a couple of occasions in our weekly meetings when I spoke over him and he gave me a look that could have sliced me in two.'

* * *

Don woke at the crack of dawn to the sound of a rooster. He lay still for a while as he collected his thoughts. He was satisfied that much progress had been made and that James in particular had had a significant breakthrough and shift in thinking. Don knew of course that the revelations and discussions on this trip would only get them to the starting blocks. The real work in bringing it all to life was yet to come.

But he also reminded himself that change of this nature starts initially with a burning platform that creates no doubt about the need to change. He was confident that the Drinkwaters already recognised that the changes in the market and their ability to adapt was a concern. But they would have to convince their team of that too.

Don also knows of the importance of winning over the hearts and minds of a workforce in a time of change. Change is not easy and some people resist that. But Don has done this many times before and was not overly concerned about that, because when the CEO of an organisation is on board with the change, the likelihood of success goes up. He was really pleased with James and he looked forward to the day ahead, with a little trepidation. He had taken risks before, but today required careful choreography.

He pondered on the face-off between James and Tom in particular. This predicament has a lot of emotion attached to it and Don's own skills as a facilitator would be tested. But he had a plan that involved an amount of risk. He reminded himself of Muhammad Ali's quote and it got the rice paper treatment.

'He who is not courageous enough to take risks will accomplish nothing in life.'

The Drinkwaters arrived at the marina to find Don throwing something into the water. 'He's at it again Clare. Seriously, I wonder about him sometimes.'

Clare smacked James' arm as she said, 'Good morning, Don!'

After settling in, Don started the engine, exited the marina and turned north towards Athlone.

'Guys I hope you don't mind, but we have a slight change in plan. I had arranged for your driver to pick you up in Portumna, which is south of here. But something has come up and I have to get back to Dublin tonight. So I'll have to make my way back to Carrick-on-Shannon before dark. I hope that's okay with you?'

'Sure,' said James. 'But does that mean we have to listen to all the same stories and history lessons for the second time?'

Don giggled and continued, 'I made a call and arranged for your driver to collect you at the Radisson Hotel in Athlone. He will be there in the afternoon. That will be plenty of time to get you back to Dublin for your night in the city before flying home tomorrow evening.'

The truth was that Don had no intention of going back to Carrick-on-Shannon that evening. He only hoped that they didn't bother to calculate the cruising time and that the river locks closed at 8 p.m. Otherwise they'd know something didn't quite add up.

BANAGHER TO ATHLONE

Although Banagher is located in the floodplain of the River Shannon, the town itself was developed on high ground and remains virtually flood-free all year round. However, this section of the river has a very shallow gradient and regularly floods parts of the surrounding countryside. Don informed his guests that the resultant wet grassland area, known as the Shannon Callows, is an internationally recognised wild bird and wildlife habitat and is classified as a special area of conservation.

'Don, we really enjoyed the craic, as you call it, last night in J.J. Hough's. What an atmosphere!' said Clare.

James added, 'When the owner's sister made her entrance and sat at the piano, she was like local royalty. I could imagine her as the Queen of Banagher.'

'The ivories on that piano are well-worn, I can assure you,' said Don. 'It's one of the most popular bars on the river. You haven't visited Ireland if you haven't been to J.J. Hough's. Not everyone gets what they're all about and you'd want to see how they respond to online reviews. It's hilarious. Check them out.'

After coming to terms with the change of plan and knowing that they had one day left together for now, James asked, 'Don we really have covered a lot in the last few days. And I have to say that I'm seeing the business and the future in a whole different light. I know that a lot has to change and much of that starts with me. But I'll admit, it's all somewhat challenging. Tell me, where do we go from here?'

Don responded, 'The first thing I have to say, in all earnest, is well done. And I don't mean that in a patronising way. You really have impressed me with your openness to feedback and acceptance of the need to change. I applaud you for that.'

'Well, thanks, I think!' said James with a slight laugh.

Don continued, 'And of course it is daunting. But I want to assure you again that, first of all, you're not the first company to be going through a culture refresh like this. There are tried and tested frameworks to ensure its success. But, of course, it requires careful planning and tailoring to make it work for GTD. As you know, we have two days booked with you and your senior team very soon. That's going to get us started.'

'I'm not sure what else you have planned for us today Don, but when James and I were chatting this morning, we made a short list of concerns that we have,' said Clare.

'That's great,' said Don. 'Let's start with that list so and I'll make sure to answer all of them. Do you mind if I take a look?'

Don scanned the list and said, 'Your questions are all spot on. But I'm surprised that you don't have anything on here about Vikings or leprechauns!' he laughed.

James laughed too, 'I suppose Don, I'm just keen to know where this culture stuff fits with strategy, structure and all other priorities?'

Don sorted the list in his mind and to help him answer their questions, he gave them an overview of the *7 Steps to Profit*. He asked James to take the wheel as he scribbled a rough drawing of a pyramid on rice paper, accompanied by seven words. He explained the seven words like this.

Step 1 is *Vision*: this is at the bottom of the pyramid. It highlights the need for having a clearly defined vision and mission. It sets context for everything that follows. It's the "*why*" a company exists and it never changes, as it defines the brand positioning. For example, Selfridges department store is very definitely a luxury brand, whereas Primark has a volume high street offering. Having that clarity of brand DNA is enormously helpful for the buyers when they go to the four corners of the world to source and curate merchandise.

Step 2 is *Culture*: this step is about having a clearly defined culture. It's the "*how*" things should get done. This too almost never changes. Culture might need tweaking from time to time, every few years, but is unlikely to have fundamental shifts. The exception might be if there is a merger or acquisition. We use values to define culture. And the four "must-have" values we have talked about over the last couple of days will get us started. They are customer-centricity, respect, accountability and agility.

Strategy is *Step 3*: that outlines the "*what*" that needs to be done to achieve the ambition. That should be updated every year.

Structure is *Step 4*: strategy is followed by structure, and elements of that too can change annually. This points to the "*who*" that will be responsible for what gets done.

Customer is *Step 5*: this step requires you to take time to build a sub-strategy around how you connect with your customer.

Step 6 is all about your *Proposition*: this is where you take time to define your product mix, your route to market and how your people should interact with your customers.

Step 7 is *Execution*: this is the day job, where organisations spend 99 percent of their time getting things done. However, a lack of adequate consideration for Steps 1–6 risks ambiguity at the execution stage, false starts, conflict and tension, and poor results.

As Don rolled up the rice paper around a hazelnut and threw it in the river, he continued, 'I'm describing these seven steps to you as if it was a linear model. But of course, it's not. For example, steps five and six are iterative. They impact each other. But you'll get the picture.'

'That is helpful,' said Clare. 'It gives me comfort to know that whatever change we embark on, it will be well-considered, structured and planned.'

After a pause, Don continued. 'Now the biggest failure would be for us to arrive back from this trip and just present these four values to your leadership team as a *fait accompli*.'

'But didn't our teams already input their ideas to the survey?' asked James.

'Yes they did James, but the detail, the wording and the plan around how to bring them to life will require their buy-in and their commitment to act them out. Think about this,' said Don. 'Firstly, after agreeing them with the senior team, we have to launch the new values with a fanfare to show the wider team that something big is happening. And your leadership team need to be involved in that, to show their teams that they are fully on board. That is just phase one, and it is a project. But then we have to roll them out over time, and that's a programme of activity.'

'Not only that,' said Clare. 'But our team are bound to have some better ideas than us. They're closer to the grassroots and they know what it will take to get everyone on board.'

'And don't forget, they're not expecting anything like this,' said Don. 'As far as they are concerned, they're scheduled to attend a two-day strategy workshop soon. But I know you agree that if we only spend time building a new strategy for the business we'd be missing so much opportunity to build real commercial value for the long term. It would be like painting over rust.'

'Or like a band-aid on an ulcer,' James quipped.

As they passed under the bridge at Shannonbridge, James slowed to 5 km/h while passing the marina and Clare put the kettle on.

'This is effectively a change programme,' said Don. 'And all change programmes go through three phases which I describe simply as, "*get ready, go, and don't stop!*" The first two phases are obvious and go without saying, but the third phase is about locking in or freezing the change, so the business doesn't fall back into its old ways.'

'So what I think you're saying Don, is that all of the concerns we expressed on our list will be carefully planned in the workshop, is that it?' asked Clare.

'Yes,' said Don. 'That's not to dismiss any of your points, but for now I want to reassure you that we'll deal with all of those questions in great detail. We'll agree a plan by bringing the full management team into the process and we'll have great debate about the key opportunities and challenges. But we'll also batten down in words that suit GTD the four values that we have discussed. Once again, they are customer-centricity, respect, accountability and agility'.

'But I would like to know now about disruption and timeframe,' said James.

'Of course,' said Don. 'Culture change like this does take time. It is definitely a programme that will continue for a number of years, and momentum needs to be maintained throughout. We have to win over the hearts and minds of everybody in the organisation. So I'd encourage you to have a cross-functional steering group of about five to seven people. That will help to minimise disruption. And in addition, you should have an internal champion or programme leader who has ready access to you to lead that steering group.'

Don had already given this a lot of thought. This "champion" needs to have a passion for the business, understand its heritage, be good with people, and have credibility with all stakeholders. He had a name in mind for the role, but kept that to himself for the moment.

James and Clare immediately started considering names of people from across the business for that role and the steering group. They fell into the trap of identifying only those who they knew would be positive and supportive.

'I think it might be a good idea to include one or two people that have alternative views too. Wouldn't it be better to have competing voices on the team, rather than a group of "yes men or women"? We'd know early on, before rollout, what the level of resistance might be like and what the issues are, and therefore we can plan around them,' said Don. James and Clare agreed.

With James' input, Clare made a list of potential candidates for this new steering group. The one name that Don had in mind was not on the list. Once again, he held his counsel.

James continued to pilot the boat northwards. He slowed appropriately as they passed the berths at Clonmacnoise. He waved at other boaters as they passed in the other direction. He took note of any navigational changes due to the positioning of red and black markers in the water. He was quite jovial and seemed to be in great form.

Don allowed some silence as they all enjoyed the beautiful scenery and surrounding bogland. Prompted by the historical structures at Clonmacnoise, they talked at length again about Irish culture and the general landscape. The Drinkwaters seemed quite smitten with it all. Between the task at hand and the comments about the surrounding environment, Don was prompted to quote an excerpt of a story written by a friend, Catherine Doyle.

Fluttering proudly,
the butterfly appreciated the results of its recent metamorphosis.
With its new skills, it could soar to new heights above the flowers
and was ready for new challenges.
Life in its previous form as a caterpillar had been good,
if a little slow.
Although it could cope well, it knew that change was inevitable.
It could never have resisted it.
So the caterpillar did what was natural
and made itself ready for an uncertain new world.
Of course, the change had not been easy,
It never is.
But now the butterfly was at last free to realise its full potential.

James and Clare both reflected on the story of the butterfly and the appropriateness of the analogy.

Don returned to the question. 'There really is a great future ahead, but there will of course be disruption. It's hard to say exactly how much disruption it will bring. But disruption sounds a little negative and let's not see it that way. I suspect that there will be some cost for internal communications, such as new collateral to help the launch, and there will be activity to create positive noise and momentum around the business. I also suspect there will be lots of workshops and training activity. But some of that can be handled by empowering and training up a small team of internal trainers.'

'I'm starting to see how it may come together,' said Clare. 'Undoubtedly, there will be lots of meetings. But I also think that they will be beneficial so long as we keep the whole thing upbeat and focused on the benefits for all,' she added.

'Yes,' said Don. 'This will make GTD a much more enjoyable and rewarding place to work. It will also dramatically improve your employer brand.'

'There's something else I'm curious about,' said James. 'You mentioned earlier that when an organisation has a clearly defined culture, then nobody can copy it. But aren't these four values that you've asked us to embrace quite generic? It's hard to argue how any organisation would not use the same ones,' he added.

'That is true,' said Don. 'But as far as I'm concerned, "the devil is in the detail" and that's how you make them your own. Let me explain. On the one hand, it's about how you interpret them for your business. And on the other hand, it's how you link them to all phases in the *7 Steps to Profit*.'

'Let's first of all look at how you interpret them,' said Don. 'Let's think of two different airlines, Emirates and Ryanair. Both of them would claim to be customer-centric. But Emirates' first-class and business-class customers will have very different expectations to Ryanair's customers, as Ryanair is a low-cost no-frills airline. The details of what customer-centricity means for both companies are polar opposite. Does that make sense?'

'Yes it does,' said James. 'Even in our B2B world, I can see how some suppliers focus on premium products and some on non-branded merchandise.'

Then Clare added, 'and I'm sure it's not just about their product offering. I'm sure it also applies to all customer touchpoints such as ordering, deliveries, etc.'

'That's totally correct,' said Don. 'And the second consideration is, as I said, how you link your values to all seven steps. For example, you might structure your business today to have sales representatives calling to customers on a regular cycle. After all, you say that the industry is a people business. Other competitors might decide to offer an online ordering service only, believing that they are being agile. Now I know that we have to explore all options and maybe even challenge some sacred cows. But you'll get the picture. If you aspire to be a premium brand, you'd find it hard to change that element of your structure, wouldn't you?'

'I get it,' said James. 'We can't look at any value in isolation, nor can we look at them without blending them with all of the seven steps.'

'Not only that,' said Clare. 'But our people are individuals. While we can give them guidance through the values for how we want them to behave, there will inevitably be differences.'

Don continued, 'You should interpret these four values appropriately for your particular organisation, the dynamics in your industry and the challenges you face in your market. After all, your heritage is unique and your business model has evolved over time. Your unique collection of personalities, stories, processes are all your own. So it's how you adapt and apply these four values to all of that, that's what will make you unique.'

After a pause, Clare added, 'the "respect" value would have a huge influence on our attitude to home-working too. I know that there are a lot of very traditional and autocratic companies in our industry. In our new culture, we might prioritise home-working as an opportunity, depending on the roles of course. But our competitors might not see it the same way.' Surprisingly, and as a measure of how much he had moved in the last 48 hours, James nodded his agreement.

ATHLONE

After much debate and excitement from the Drinkwaters, Don thought about the next few hours. Early that morning he had planned to meet a client in Athlone at 3 p.m. He hadn't yet told James and Clare but was sure they wouldn't mind. It would give them an opportunity to have some private time in the town without him.

They arrived at Athlone Lock and were lucky to find the gates open on their approach. James slowed and navigated the boat straight in without having to moor beforehand. They chatted amongst themselves as they acclimatised to the different sounds of the bustling town. When the water levels rose and the gates opened on the far side, Don took over the controls.

He steered the boat onwards under the bridge and headed towards the moorings at the Radisson Hotel on the east bank of the river. The calm was interrupted by roars of delight and hilarity that they couldn't ignore. Just then, James heard his name being called in an accent that wasn't local. To their left, they saw their German acquaintances moored to the river wall. Their boat, with several fishing rods hanging over the side, was bustling with activity. And a crowd of locals and other boaters were gathered around.

Don gently steered his boat broadside to the Germans and shackled them together. To loud applause and cheers from the local anglers, one of the Germans proudly held a very large salmon aloft.

'James, look! I caught the biggest salmon ever! More than 12 kgs!' he shouted.

'That's over 20 lbs to you, being a Brexiteer!' laughed Don.

'Congratulations!' shouted James, Clare and Don, as they too clapped and cheered. James opened his phone to take photographs.

'It's more like the Lough Ree Monster, if you ask me,' said a local, to much laughter from his friends. 'Look at the strange golden hue off it!' said another. 'Maybe it's the Salmon of Knowledge?'

With that comment, James nearly dropped his phone into the river. He glared at a smirking Don. Clare also glared at a smirking Don. Don looked back at James and then he looked at Clare. The three burst into laughter as Don pursed his lips, slowly raised his hands in the air and said, "There you go! Welcome to Ireland!"

In the midst of laughter, James added, 'so that's what the rice paper and hazelnuts were for!'

After celebrating with the Germans for a short while, Don traversed the river and moored at the Radisson Hotel. He suggested to his guests that they have lunch in the Radisson. 'That's good,' said James. 'Looking at that salmon has made me peckish!'

Don was a little distracted. He had butterflies in his stomach, due to the plans he had made for the rest of the day. It required delicate handling and he was very concerned about ensuring everything went smoothly. He had arranged for his other clients to meet him in the hotel at 3 p.m.

They entered the hotel and Don guided James and Clare to the Quayside Bar and Lounge, as he himself stopped for a moment to greet Manager Gavan Feighery. After a few quiet words, he re-joined his guests and they ordered a light lunch.

Over salad and sandwiches, they agreed a schedule for the following weeks. They had already planned to have the two-day initial workshop with the leadership team, but Don agreed to arrive in twenty-four hours earlier to fine-tune the objectives, the agenda and the break-out sessions.

'I'm very much looking forward to what happens next,' said James.

'I am too,' said Clare. 'And I know there will be lots of challenges along the way, but I'm feeling good about our approach and our plan.'

'Yes,' said Don. 'The steps in managing change have been tried and tested countless times before. The secret here is in the quality of planning and getting all stakeholders on board. And we'll put extra effort into this so as to ensure we deliver a fantastic programme of change. I'm very confident that we're on the right track. So, are we all agreed?' he asked.

'Absolutely,' said James and Clare as they all gave each other high-fives.

Clare added, 'Having Sarah and Tom back on board would top it all off. I honestly think that if they realised how determined we are, they'd feel differently.'

James looked down at his hands and then announced, 'Clare, the first thing I'm going to do when we get home is to call them both and ask to meet them. I know we're meeting for dinner for my birthday in ten days, but I don't want to wait that long.'

'That's a really great idea,' said Clare enthusiastically.

When they were finished, Don said 'I hope you don't mind, but I've arranged to meet someone at 3 p.m. I won't be long but I have arranged with Gavan for you to see the river from the best room in the house. The view from the fourth floor is spectacular. Let me introduce you to him. He'll also tell you about his business and the world of hospitality in Ireland.'

Don introduced James and Clare to Gavan and left them as they headed for the elevator. James asked Gavan lots of questions about business and what new trends were emerging. After showing them the view, Gavan left them alone to enjoy it and to chat over fresh coffees.

Meanwhile, Don climbed the stairs to the third floor and entered one of the conference rooms. Waiting for him were his two clients. Although it wasn't their first time to meet Don, they both looked nervous. They expressed once again their anxieties about what brought them to this point but they also expressed their hopes for the future. Don put them at ease as best he could by telling them reassuring stories of triumph over adversity, and he said, 'I promise, everything *will* work out for the best.'

After twenty minutes, Don said, 'Let's go!'

* * *

James and Clare were just about to sit down when there was a gentle knock and the door opened. Standing at the doorway were Sarah and Tom. After the initial shock, Clare ran across the room and hugged them both. Sarah then reached for her stunned father to join them. James gave Sarah a bear-hug. Then he stepped closer to Tom and embraced him like he would never let him go. No words were spoken. And even if there were, they wouldn't have been heard through the tears.

Don left the family alone for twenty more minutes and, eventually, he tentatively joined them in their room. Realising that the mood was ecstatic, he exhaled and joined in with their banter.

He then outlined the plans for the rest of the day. He told his guests that they were actually booked into the hotel for the night but that he would leave them on their own to chat and catch up. 'In the meantime, why don't we take a short trip and show Sarah and Tom the Lough Ree Monster?'

Sarah and Tom looked at him sceptically as James said through the laughter, 'Come on. I'll tell you all about it. And don't forget, Don is an Irishman who has undoubtedly kissed the Blarney Stone!'

They all boarded the boat. Don gave the keys to James and asked him to take control, which he proudly did. James explained the controls to Tom as he said, 'Maybe it's time for a new toy on the Birmingham canals!' Don wound the rope at the stern and hung it on the cleat. As James pulled away slowly from the mooring, Don stepped off the transom back onto the mooring and said, 'You go ahead guys, I'll see you back here in a couple of hours. James you know what you're doing and where you're going. Call if you need me.'

Clare knew exactly what Don was doing. She appreciated his thoughtfulness and gave him a wink and a warm smile. After miming the words 'Thank you', she said, 'see you soon, Don. I really think you should write a book on this stuff!'

'Funny you should say that, I even have the name ready!' said Don as she watched him take the last piece of rice paper and edible ink pen from his pocket. He waved it at Clare and then started to write something. After just three letters '*Dar...*', the ink ran out.

He shrugged his shoulders and walked back to the hotel, singing a few lines of Louis Armstrong's 'What a Wonderful World' to himself.

DON'S RICE-PAPER QUOTES

'Customer satisfaction is a key driver of long-term business results.'

'Customer experience is the new battleground.'

'Organisational culture is often defined as "the way we do things around here", including actions, behaviours and words.'

'Others may copy your strategy, but no one can copy your culture.'

'Keep in mind the lifetime potential of each customer, rather than just the value of today's transaction.'

'Put the customer at the heart of everything that you do – front and centre of all decision-making.'

'Premium is the New Black.'

'Achieving long-lasting change of culture is not a project. It's a programme.'

'To gain respect, you have to show respect.'

'There is no contradiction between seeking maximum productivity and high levels of engagement.'

'Respect should be remembered in all elements of the HR mix; that includes right person – right job, training, communications and wellbeing.'

Culture Matters

'Leaders who show respect build more trust – and engagement follows, leading to high productivity.'

'Budgets are not plans.'

'Objectives without metrics (that include quality and quantity metrics, along with a timeframe) are a "get out of jail free" card.'

'Reward and consequences are essential enablers of accountability.'

'Digital disruptors change the dynamic in an industry. You can embrace it or ignore it. Coping with it is up to you.'

'The volume, the complexity and the speed of change demands an agile culture, otherwise you get left behind.'

'He who is not courageous enough to take risks will accomplish nothing in life.' (Muhammad Ali)

7 STEPS TO PROFIT

1. *Brand DNA*
2. *Culture*
3. *Strategy*
4. *Structure*
5. *Customer*
6. *Proposition*
7. *Execution*